Tax evasion is an old but growing problem. It raises issues relevant to a broad range of social sciences – accounting, economics, psychology, political science, and sociology – and is of enormous importance in policy design.

But research into tax evasion has been beset with measurement problems; the hidden economy is well named.

This book seeks to demonstrate that experimental methods provide a potentially powerful approach which can complement existing methods such as the use of surveys and official records. The key is to design experimental situations that engage the same psychological processes as their real-world counterparts. The authors, drawn from backgrounds in law as well as social and economic psychology, describe and evaluate this distinctive approach to tax evasion through consideration of work carried out in both the Netherlands and the UK over the last four years.

European Monographs in Social Psychology

Tax evasion

European Monographs in Social Psychology

Executive Editors:
J. RICHARD EISER and KLAUS R. SCHERER
Sponsored by the European Association of Experimental Social Psychology

This series, first published by Academic Press (who will continue to distribute the numbered volumes), appeared under the joint imprint of Cambridge University Press and the Maison des Sciences de l'Homme in 1985 as an amalgamation of the Academic Press series and the European Studies in Social Psychology, published by Cambridge and the Maison in collaboration with the Laboratoire Européen Psychologie Sociale of the Maison.

The original aims of the two series still very much apply today: to provide a forum for the best European research in different fields of social psychology and to foster the interchange of the ideas between different developments and different traditions. The executive Editors also expect that it will have an important role to play as a European forum for international work.

Other titles in this series:

Unemployment by Peter Kelvin and Joanna E. Jarrett
National characteristics by Dean Peabody
Experiencing emotion by Klaus R. Scherer, Harald G. Wallbott and Angela B. Summerfield
Levels of explanation in social psychology by Willem Doise
Understanding attitudes to the European Community: a social-psychological study in four member states by Miles Hewstone
Arguing and thinking: a rhetorical approach to social psychology by Michael Billig
Non-verbal communication in depression by Heiner Ellgring
Social representations of intelligence by Gabriel Mugny and Felice Carugati
Speech and reasoning in everyday life by Uli Windisch
Account episodes. The management or escalation of conflict by Peter Schönbach
The ecology of the self: relocation and self-concept change by Stefan E. Hormuth
Situation cognition and coherence in personality: An individual-centred approach by Barbara Krahé
Explanations, accounts and illusions: a critical analysis by John McClure

SUPPLEMENTARY VOLUMES

Talking politics: a psychological framing for views from youth in Britain by Kum-Kum Bhavnani

Tax evasion

An experimental approach

Paul Webley
Lecturer in psychology, University of Exeter

Henry Robben
Lecturer in economic psychology, Tilburg University

Henk Elffers
Lecturer in research methods, Faculty of Law, Erasmus University, Rotterdam

Dick Hessing
Senior lecturer in sociology of law, Erasmus University, Rotterdam,
and Professor of psychology and law, University of Leyden

with Frank A. Cowell, Susan B. Long,
and Judyth A. Swingen

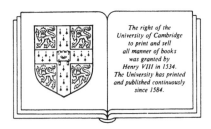

The right of the
University of Cambridge
to print and sell
all manner of books
was granted by
Henry VIII in 1534.
The University has printed
and published continuously
since 1584.

Cambridge University Press
Cambridge
New York   Port Chester   Melbourne   Sydney

Editions de la Maison des Sciences de l'Homme
Paris

CAMBRIDGE UNIVERSITY PRESS
Cambridge, New York, Melbourne, Madrid, Cape Town, Singapore,
São Paulo, Delhi, Dubai, Tokyo

Cambridge University Press
The Edinburgh Building, Cambridge CB2 8RU, UK

With Editions de la Maison des Sciences de l'Homme
54 Boulevard Raspail, 75270 Paris Cedex 06, France

Published in the United States of America by Cambridge University Press, New York

www.cambridge.org
Information on this title: www.cambridge.org/9780521130615

First published 1991
This digitally printed version 2010

A catalogue record for this publication is available from the British Library

Library of Congress Cataloguing in Publication data
Tax evasion: an experimental approach. / Paul Webley . . . [et al.].
    p.   cm. – (European monographs in social psychology)
Includes bibliographical references and index.
ISBN 0 521 37459 6
1. Tax evasion – Great Britain – Psychological aspects. 2. Tax evasion –
Netherlands – Psychological aspects. I. Webley, Paul.
II. Series.
HJ2348.7.G7I38   1991
336.2′06 – dc20   90–24640   CIP

ISBN 978-0-521-37459-0 Hardback
ISBN 978-0-521-13061-5 Paperback

To our parents and the memory of our parents

Contents

Preface   *page* xiii
Acknowledgements   xv

1 Tax evasion in theory and in practice   1
  1.1 Introduction   1
    1.1.1 The size and scope of the problem: Estimates and
      guesstimates from around the world   3
    1.1.2 Policy issues   7
  1.2 Why do people evade taxes? Man as a rational amoral
    taxpayer   8
  1.3 Why do people evade taxes? Social psychological views   13
    1.3.1 Lewis (1982): Individuals and authorities   13
    1.3.2 Smith and Kinsey (1987): Tax decisions in a social
      context   15
    1.3.3 Groenland and Van Veldhoven (1983): Personality
      and situational characteristics as determinants of
      evasion   17
    1.3.4 Vogel (1974): A social psychological typology of
      taxpayers   17
    1.3.5 An attribution approach to tax evasion   18
    1.3.6 Weigel, Hessing, and Elffers (1987): Tax evasion as
      defective behaviour within a social dilemma 19
  1.4 The wider social context: The importance of norms,
  cultural rules, and differences in tax systems   23

2 The problem of measurement   29
  2.1 Introduction   29
    2.1.1 Sources of data   29
    2.1.2 Indirect data   30
    2.1.3 Data from official files   31
    2.1.4 Self-reported data   33
    2.1.5 Combined data   36
  2.2 The experimental approach   39

2.2.1 The experimental approach: A wider perspective 44
2.3 A first example, UK04: Tax evasion in a small-business
  simulation 48
2.4 Conclusions 53

3 **Social comparison, equity, attitudes, and tax evasion** 55
3.1 Introduction 55
  3.1.1 Equity and tax evasion 55
  3.1.2 Social comparison and tax evasion 57
  3.1.3 Individual differences in the predisposition to evade 58
3.2 UK05: The effect of inequity and earnings comparisons on
  evasion 60
3.3 UK06: Effects of social comparison and inequity on
  evasion 63
3.4 UK07: Social comparison and correlates of evasion 69
3.5 NL01: Social comparison and correlates of evasion 72
3.6 Conclusions 77

4 **Framing, opportunity, and individual differences** 79
4.1 Theoretical background 79
  4.1.1 Framing 79
  4.1.2 Opportunity 85
4.2 Two studies into the opportunity to evade 86
  4.2.1 UK08: Opportunity, audit probability, and values 86
  4.2.2 UK09: Opportunity, audit probability, alienation,
    and attitudes towards the law 90
4.3 Introduction to the improved simulations 92
  4.3.1 Overview of instructions 92
4.4 NL02: Withholding, opportunity, and attitudes 99
4.5 NL03: Withholding, opportunity, and attitudes 102
4.6 NL04: Decision frames and opportunity 105
4.7 UK10 and UK11: Decision frames and opportunity 107
4.8 Correlational analyses 109
4.9 Conclusions 112

5 **The subjects' view** 114
5.1 Introduction 114
5.2 Postexperimental questionnaires 115
5.3 Postexperimental interviews 117

6 **Tax-evasion experiments: An economist's view** 123
FRANK A. COWELL

Contents   xi

7 **The conduct of tax-evasion experiments: Validation, analytical methods, and experimental realism**   128
SUSAN B. LONG AND JUDYTH A. SWINGEN
7.1 Some methodological issues in the analysis of experimental data   128
  7.1.1 Random assignment and equivalent groups   129
  7.1.2 Exploiting within-group and cross-time variation in evasion behaviours   131
7.2 Reflections in the light of US experience   135
  7.2.1 Tax avoidance and evasion as substitute behaviours 135
  7.2.2 Tax noncompliance versus tax evasion   136
  7.2.3 The impact of complexity and opportunity on taxpayer compliance   137

8 **Reply and conclusions**   139
8.1 The expected return of evading taxes   139
8.2 The existence of hard-core nonevaders   140
8.3 Keep them simple?   142
8.4 Conclusions   143

References   145
Subject index   156
Author index   158

Preface

This book is the record of a collective intellectual journey. We began research in tax evasion for very different reasons. PW wanted an excuse to teach himself how to program; the original experimental studies of tax evasion appeared well suited to implementation on a micro-computer and so after a Christmas vacation largely spent staring at a VDU a primitive simulation came into being. HR came to Exeter on a research placement and, offered the choice between working on gift-giving or tax evasion, opted, for some unaccountable reason, for evasion. HE and DH's motivation was purer; having developed a theoretical model to account for organ donation, they were looking for fresh empirical fields for their model to conquer.

But it is a psychological commonplace that we need different analyses to account for why people start indulging in a behaviour (be it smoking, gambling, or researching into tax evasion) and why they continue. The addictive properties of research may be less well known than those of nicotine but they are equally powerful. In this case the glazed eyes and shaking hands were the result of long hours at the keyboard as we became obsessive about devising experiments that were realistic and involving and convinced that such experiments were good for you.

It has to be said that this was a minority view. When we tell people that we do research into tax evasion they usually laugh and say something like 'well, you must tell me how to evade mine'. Our colleagues in psychology treat us even less seriously: tax evasion is seen as a minor problem of peripheral interest to psychologists, and our chosen approach, an experimental one, as inappropriate. One aim of this book, then, is to persuade them otherwise. More generally, we want to show how the kinds of studies we describe here can make a contribution to both social psychology and economics and play a part in the further development of economic psychology.

There have been some secondary gains from working on the book. PW can now hold a halting conversation in Dutch (of the 'two lagers please' kind) and has memorised certain key phrases (the one to remember is 'Dick betaalt'). HR has extended his already considerable grasp of English with some equally useful phrases ('I'm just off to point Percy at the porcelain'). HE claims he has learned that it is possible to simulate co-authorship without doing any real work. More convincingly, DH argues he has found some unexplored ways to evade taxes.

It is unusual for authors to ask their readers to be patient with them at the outset (although perhaps more should) but with two audiences in mind, social psychologists and economists, we feel we should. Economists will no doubt consider our descriptions of economic theory oversimplified; social psychologists will probably regard much of what we say about method as fairly routine. But we hope that there is something here for everyone and that, as a result, economists and psychologists will be seen more often in each other's offices, conferences and journals.

Acknowledgements

This project is like many others in at least one important respect. The 'without-whom' department is generously filled with nice people, without whom this book would have been much more difficult to write. We also think the quality would have suffered 'without whom'. Perhaps most significantly, they all contributed to the pleasure we experienced when working on the book.

Many people have helped in a variety of ways. Several have assisted in collecting the experimental data, for which we are greatly indebted. Marion van Engelen and Lucette Klein Tank helped us in the Netherlands; Gary Calderwood, Peter Jensen, Anne Mattock, and Ira Morris provided excellent service in Exeter. Gary Calderwood also read drafts of the first two chapters. In Exeter, Rachel Kirby has sorted out our BASIC computer programs for a number of years and Andy Black wrote the BASIC translation of the program used in chapter 4. The interviews reported in chapter 5 were transcribed by Julie Dawick. The secretarial staff of the Exeter psychology department dealt with our demands with unfailing patience and courtesy. Our colleagues, both in our departments and in the wider academic community, have also been very helpful, in particular Dick Eiser, Stephen Lea, and Alan Lewis. Most of all we must thank the people who took part.

The whole process was made possible through the financial and technical support of the Department of Psychology of the University of Exeter, the British Academy, the British Council, the Nuffield Foundation, and the Faculty of Law of Erasmus University. They provided us with the necessary infrastructure to carry out the reported research in relative peace and independence.

We would like to thank Elsevier-North Holland for permission to reprint Tables 2.1, 2.2, and 2.3, and some associated text which first appeared in P. Webley, Audit probabilities and tax evasion in a business simulation, *Economics Letters*, 25 (1987), 267–70.

Some of our studies were carried out as part of a large international collaboration. During two workshops on our subject, organised at Erasmus University, we were lucky to receive insightful comments and ideas, probably many of which we did not use as their originators intended. We express our thanks to Russell H. Weigel, Karl-Erik Wärneryd, Richard Wahlund, John T. Scholz, Karyl A. Kinsey, Susan B. Long, Luk Van Langenhove, and Francisco Alvira Martin.

The manuscript has benefited profoundly from the comments we received from Frank A. Cowell, Susan B. Long, and Judyth A. Swingen. They have read the manuscript with meticulous care, and indicated how experimental research into tax evasion can gain in strength and improve in precision. Their ideas are represented in two separate chapters in this text. We are very happy that they responded affirmatively to our request to comment on the book, and, moreover, for a job well done.

The book was conceived while Paul Webley was on sabbatical leave at Erasmus University, Rotterdam. He is grateful for its hospitality and financial support.

1 Tax evasion in theory and in practice

1.1 Introduction

Taxation and evasion have always gone together and income-tax evasion –
the subject of this monograph – is as old as income tax itself. In fact, in
William Pitt's speech introducing income tax in Britain in 1799, the problem
of evasion occupied centre stage. It was 'to prevent all evasion and fraud' that
'a general tax shall be imposed on all the leading branches of income' (Wright
1819). Ironically, even though tax rates in Victorian England were set at
levels that now seem unbelievably low (when reintroduced in the 1942
budget, income tax was set at 2.9%), there were complaints about evasion
from the outset. In 1866 it was estimated that the average taxable income
declared was less than half what it should have been. In Exeter, where there
was a special report in 1871, only 20% of those liable to income tax made
returns that were satisfactory to the Revenue Service (Sabine 1966).

So income-tax evasion *per se* is not a modern problem. But the sheer scale of
the public sector in most economies today makes it a much more pressing
one. It is important economically: the most recent direct estimates in the
United States by the Internal Revenue Service, for example, put the cost of
federal income-tax evasion at 85 billion dollars (IRS 1988a). It is important
to individuals: before the second world war less than 20% of the British
workforce and only 4% of the American paid income tax, figures that rose in a
few years to 66% and 51% respectively (Goode 1976). There is some evidence
that the amount of evasion is increasing in America (Etzioni 1986) and it
seems as if anti-tax sentiment has been growing in the past decade. Opinion
polls in the States and the UK show a marked increase in tax resistance; a
1973 Harris poll revealed that 31% of respondents felt that federal income
taxes were reasonable, a figure that had dropped to 20% by 1978. An IRS
survey immediately after the passage of the Tax Reform Act 1986 (TRA 86)
showed that 28% thought the new law would be more fair. However, in a
1988 follow-up this percentage had dropped to 17 after people had actually
had to deal with the law (Broehm & Sharp 1989). After TRA 86 three-
quarters of the subjects in three different surveys expressed the sentiment
that the tax burdens imposed on middle-income individuals were too high
(McKee & Gerbing 1989; Swingen 1989).

1

Tax resistance and evasion are not necessarily bad of course. Tax resistance has a long and honourable history. Two examples dear to our hearts are the Peasant's Revolt in England in 1381, which was provoked by the imposition of a new poll tax, and the Dutch war of independence from Spain, which was partly sparked off by the introduction of a new centralised tax system by the Habsburgs. Even today evasion need not be economically detrimental. As Bracewell-Milnes (1979) put it, 'an economy breathes through its tax loopholes'. He pointed out that it is possible for the suppression of evasion to lead to losses to the government as well as to the individuals concerned. This would be the case if the alternative to evasion is a shift to an activity which results in less government revenue rather than proper payment of taxes on the initial earnings.

But here we are not concerned with the moral or economic rights and wrongs of the issue. Our aim in this book is to introduce a new way of exploring an old but growing problem. For a social psychologist, evasion is an interesting real-life form of cheating which may be treated as a social dilemma. It may be explained through people's attitudes, by reference to social comparison and aspects of decision making. For an economic psychologist it is a paradigm case of the interaction of the individual and the wider economy. Finally, for the economist it is an intriguing part of the national economy which is outside the national accounts. We hope to say something to all these people. But in this chapter we aim simply to set the scene with some descriptive background and a consideration of why people evade taxes.

First, some definitions. In legal terms there is a distinction between tax avoidance and tax evasion. Avoidance involves 'every attempt by legal means to prevent or reduce tax liability which would otherwise be incurred, by taking advantage of some provision or lack of provision in the law . . . it presupposes the existence of alternatives, one of which would result in less tax than the other' (Report of the Royal Commission on Taxation 1966, 538). Evasion is illegal. It can involve acts of commission or omission. So one of us may claim to have earned less in royalties from this book than is actually the case (optimistically assuming this to be worthwhile!) or simply fail to tell the revenue authorities about certain assets.

Cutting across this legal definition is the distinction between compliance and noncompliance. Researchers have often used the term 'noncompliance' to characterise the intentional or unintentional failure of taxpayers to pay their taxes correctly. Noncompliance is a more neutral term than evasion since it does not assume that an inaccurate tax return is necessarily the result of an intention to defraud the authorities and it recognises that inaccuracy may actually result in overpayment of taxes. A taxpayer may genuinely forget some extra earnings or that some expenses are tax deductible, miscalculate or simply not understand aspects of the tax form. By contrast, a term like 'tax cheating' describes deliberate acts of noncompliance and does not entail the difficulty of legal proof of tax evasion.

Do these distinctions matter? The answer has to be a cautious 'yes'. Although the reasons for intentional evasion and intentional avoidance may be very similar (i.e. to pay less tax), psychologically (and economically) we believe them to be very different. In evading tax one is knowingly breaking the law. This has social and psychological consequences such as stigma and guilt and involves confronting different costs since there is a risk of being caught and fined or sent to prison. We are obviously interested primarily in evasion. Now in practice it is difficult, if not impossible, to be certain about intent and so often we have to talk about noncompliance. The psychology of tax forms (James, Lewis & Allison 1987) and the problems caused by legal complexity (Long & Swingen 1988), although interesting, are not our main concerns here.

1.1.1 The size and scope of the problem: Estimates and guesstimates from around the world

The distinction between evasion and noncompliance is also relevant when we consider the size and scope of the problem. Noncompliance is obviously easier to estimate than evasion, though neither can be said to be easy to measure. Estimating the size of any illegal activity, be it delinquency in general or tax evasion in particular, is never easy and the differences in tax systems, the nature of economic activity and the quality of accounting make comparisons between countries difficult.

None the less we will describe some of the better-known results here and reserve a discussion of problems of measurement until the next chapter. Two direct methods and a variety of indirect methods have been used to estimate the extent of evasion. Of the direct methods, one relies on official records, the other on self-report. The first involves an intensive audit of a sample of taxpayers which is then grossed-up to reach an estimate of overall evasion. The Victorian reports mentioned above are an early example of this method. In the 1866 report, 200 cases were examined and in 40% of these fraud was judged to have taken place. A more modern example is the American Taxpayer Compliance Measurement Program (TCMP), which has involved samples of approximately 50,000 individual tax returns at intervals of two to four years since 1963. Here the scale of evasion has been more modest, although it must be remembered that some evasion occurs through no return being made (Kinsey 1984). The second involves asking people, for example using a questionnaire or telephone interview, whether they have evaded taxes and, if so, how much and how often. This can be a direct question or involve using a sealed envelope, randomised response, or a 'locked' box technique (all methods of guaranteeing the anonymity of the respondents). American self-report studies, which are summarised by Kinsey (1984), reveal noncompliance rates of between 9% and 33%.

The indirect methods can all be characterised as 'guesstimates'. Here, the size of the 'underground' economy is estimated by the traces it leaves in the official economy. Cowell (1990) likens this to trying to work out the number of moles in a field by counting the number of molehills! A variety of methods have been tried. These have included such indicators as the percentage of bank notes issued that are of large denomination and the divergence between income and expenditure estimates of the gross domestic product (GDP, which is basically the sum of income from property and income from employment). The first rests on the assumption that people try to conceal their underground economy activities by making payments in cash. For example, the increase in the ratio of cash to money held in bank accounts observed in the US since 1937–41 is attributed to the growth in the hidden economy. If it is assumed that there was no evasion in 1937–41 this leads to an estimate that the hidden economy comprised around 10% of gross national product (GNP) in 1976 (Guttman 1977) (GNP is GDP plus property income received from abroad and minus property income to foreigners). The logic of the discrepancy method is rather different; this is based on the fact that GNP can be estimated from the income side (essentially from tax records) and completely independently from the expenditure side (from household and industrial surveys). These different methods have led to divergent estimates; in the United States from 3.4% to 5% of GNP (Tanzi, cited in Maital 1982) to 25 to 33% of GNP (Feige 1979). Clearly these guesstimates have to be treated with caution.

Cowell (1990) provides a summary listing of all the main studies, whether using direct or indirect methods. He concludes that there is a consensus that the underground economy is about 2 to 10% of GNP in Western economies, with perhaps 7 to 10% being a reasonable estimate for the US (though he cautions that this conclusion should be heavily qualified). This gives us an idea of the general economic importance of the underground economy.

For a more detailed picture of the position in the Netherlands and in Britain we can rely on two recent comprehensive reviews (Smith 1986; Van Eck & Kazemier 1988). Van Eck and Kazemier summarise past research carried out in the Netherlands in the late 1970s and 1980s. This research has used both indirect methods (e.g. Broesterhuizen 1985) and surveys (Van Eck & Kazemier 1985). This gives estimates ranging from 1% to 22% of GDP, with the average being about 5% to 7%. The lowest estimates come from survey work, probably because this is only concerned with hidden income from labour (i.e. does not include the self-employed). None the less this 1% is shared by more than 1 million individuals (nearly 12% of the population).

Smith (1986) explores British evidence from the demand for cash, from national accounts discrepancies and from survey discrepancies. He concludes that, on balance, the level of underground economy activity is unlikely to be less than 3% or more than 5% of GDP, with the lower estimate being probably more accurate.

Aggregate information of this kind is, however, not enough. Ideally we would like to know the number of people who evade, how often they evade (including the number of evasions in a lifetime), how they evade (false deductions and/or underdeclaring income, etc.), the distribution of the amount evaded (e.g. do most people evade rather trivial amounts?). On the other side of the coin some comparable information (how many people are, and how much money is, involved in the deterrence process) would also be helpful. Many studies simply do not have such detailed data but we can sketch an outline picture.

In general, survey studies ask if a respondent has ever overstated deductions or underreported income. On this basis, and using only those studies that have asked a direct question or used a sealed envelope, about 25% of the American population admit that they have evaded tax at least once. This suggests that in any given year a somewhat lower percentage will be evading. The TCMP results show far more noncompliance although net undercompliance (percent undercompliance minus percent overcompliance) ranges from 26% to 35%. This suggests that, for the US at least, a working estimate of a quarter of the population annually evading tax is plausible. The evidence we have for other countries suggests that this is a reasonable 'ballpark' figure. In the Netherlands, Groenland and Van Veldhoven (1983) found that one third of their wage-earners and two-thirds of their self-employed sample reported experience of the underground economy and Van Bijsterveld (1980) tells us that two out of three entrepreneurs evaded taxes in a given year. Using a more representative sample, Hessing, Robben, and Elffers (1989) found that 11% of their Dutch respondents admitted tax evasion. Wärneryd and Walerud (1982), in a telephone survey of Swedish males, report that 19% of their sample said that they had evaded at least once. Laurin (1986), reporting on a very large-scale interview study of a representative sample of the Swedish population, singled out opportunity as a prime cause of evasion. From his results it appears that more than 30% of the Swedish population have cheated in connection with reporting their income, while 12% have claimed higher deductions than they were entitled to.

To answer the question of 'how' people evade, we can use Kinsey's (1984) detailed overview of the survey literature. When direct questions were used, 5 to 7% of respondents said that they had overstated deductions. By way of contrast, 12 to 15% admitted underreporting income. The figures in the studies that used locked box and randomised response methods are rather different, but in most cases underreporting income was the more popular form of evasion. In addition, some people evade tax by not filing returns. In the few (all American) studies that have examined this, 4% to 7% admit failure to file returns (Kinsey 1984).

The TCMP results also give some indication of the number of people evading significant amounts. The figures are obviously different from survey to survey, but from the 1979 figures 10% of the 35% net undercompliant returns were trivially noncompliant (less than $50 tax change). Some detailed Dutch data also suggest that most noncompliance detected by careful auditing is for relatively small amounts (Elffers, Robben & Hessing 1991 report that the mean tax correction was approximately £300). Looked at from the other side, Van Eck and Kazemier's (1988) large survey of hidden labour in the Netherlands suggests that the average participant earns approximately 2,300 guilders a year: 55% earn less than 1,500 guilders a year (roughly £10 a week) and only 4% earn more than 7,000 guilders a year. Brown, Levin, Rosa, and Ulph (1984), in a survey study of British taxpayers, also report that most tax evasion by the employed is for relatively small amounts. Under the Pay As You Earn (PAYE) system the chance of evading tax is limited and Brown *et al.* conclude that there is little evidence of evasion on people's main jobs. About 5% of their respondents had second jobs and 17% of these were reckoned to be evading tax on these earnings. These second-job earnings averaged approximately £18 per week (average main earnings in the survey were £92 per week).

Information on how many people are involved in the deterrence process is also hard to come by. For 1988, 8,859 officials were working at the income-tax department of the Dutch Tax Service. Of these, 2,070 were actively involved with the assessment of income on the basis of returns including desk auditing. Another 1,372 were engaged in in-depth auditing of business income. In comparison we observe that about 5 million tax returns were processed in 1988. A different perspective is obtained by looking at the cost of deterrence. The total costs of the Internal Revenue Service in the US in 1974 were $1.3 billion, which is about 0.55% of the amount of tax collected. The UK system is much more expensive; for the same year the collection costs were 1.75% of the amount collected (Barr, James & Prest 1977). Much of this money is spent on collection and data processing, though Erekson and Sullivan (1988) say that auditing accounted for 36% of the IRS budget in 1976. Of more significance is the fact that in the US only a sample of returns is audited; approximately 1,250,000 out of 96 million in 1986 (US Bureau of the Census 1987). This overall figure masks considerable variation; people with low incomes are much less likely to be audited but those with very high incomes are likely to be audited twice every three years. Erekson and Sullivan (1988) conclude that the IRS is trying to ensure compliance but is also involved in budget-constrained revenue maximisation. In the Netherlands all returns are audited, but with varying depth of audit. There are no separate phases of arithmetical checking or preprocessing; all these things are merged into one task. In the US all individual returns, although not audited, are subject to maths and clerical error checking, and computer screening for audit potential when they are received at IRS Service Centers.

1.1.2 Policy issues

Social scientific research into taxation inevitably touches on issues of policy. Tax reform has been a notable feature of government policy in a number of countries recently (Denmark, Britain, the Netherlands, and the US, to name but four). Although this has been mainly based on the desire to reduce distortions caused by taxation, for example, the effects of high marginal rates of tax on incentives to work, there have been other motives. These include a desire to simplify tax systems and, through simplification and the reduction in marginal tax rates, to bring about a reduction in tax evasion. For instance, several recent income-tax reforms have put explicit limitations on what deductions are allowable (Hagemann, Jones & Montador 1988).

Tax reform has often been based on the prevalent ideology. When it is based on research, this is usually from economics rather than other social sciences. Our own work has limited, but definite, policy implications which we will discuss in later chapters. Here we would like just to give a single example of a piece of noneconomic research with policy implications. Schwartz and Orleans (1967) examined the comparative effectiveness of the threat of legal sanctions and appeals to conscience. They obtained tax-compliance figures for three groups of taxpayers, a threat group, an appeals to conscience group and a control group. All members of these groups were interviewed about political and tax issues a month before they made their tax return. The questions that they were asked were themselves the experimental manipulation. They stressed either sanctions or personal responsibility. The tax records showed a mean change in income declaration of \$181 in the sanctions group, \$804 in the conscience group and \$87 in the control group. The sanctions group also increased their claims for tax-deductible allowances, which suggests that threats may actually increase tax avoidance or evasion. This difference approached statistical significance ($p < 0.10$) in the direction opposite of that predicted. In view of these outcomes, Schwartz and Orleans' endorsement of the capacity of threats of punishment to reduce tax evasion seems unjustified and the overall assessment of the deterrence value of civil and criminal penalties remains uncertain.

This study does not, of course, show that appeals to conscience are necessarily a better way of reducing evasion than threats. But it does suggest that a simple application of elementary economic models may be counterproductive. It is to these models that we now turn.

1.2   Why do people evade taxes? Man as a rational amoral taxpayer

If we were to stop a person in the street and ask him or her why people evade tax, the answer would almost certainly be 'greed'. Stripped of its moral connotations, that is also the basis of the answer that economists have given. The assumption is that people will commit an offence, any offence, if by so doing they maximise their utility. Becker (1968) argues that people become criminals not because their motivations are different from others' but because their costs and benefits differ. Applied to the tax situation, this treats people as rational amoral decision makers whose aim, in this as in all other areas, is simply to maximise utility. The classic model (Allingham & Sandmo 1972; see also Cowell 1985) is extremely simple. It assumes that behaviour is influenced by factors such as the tax rate (which determines the benefits of evasion) and the penalties for fraud and the probability of detection (which determine the costs). Individuals have a choice of how much income to declare and may report none, some, or all of it.

This model produces generally unsurprising predictions. For instance, an increase in penalty rate and an increase in the probability of detection both result in more income being declared. But simultaneously, with penalties on *tax* evaded rather than income concealed and decreasing absolute risk aversion – both reasonable possibilities – the model predicts that evasion *decreases* when the tax rate rises. It is not quite as simple as has sometimes been claimed; in addition to allowing predictions like the latter one, Allingham and Sandmo incorporate the nonmonetary variable 'reputation' and the notion of risk aversion into their model as well as briefly exploring the dynamic case. Though here the predictions are also fairly commonplace, e.g. in a dynamic model where discovery of evasion leads to auditing of past tax returns, income declarations increase as the years go by.

The classic model predicts that both probability of detection and the severity of penalties will affect evasion; if detection is likely and penalties severe people will be more compliant. Kinsey's (1984) review suggests that for criminal behaviour in general, penalties are less of a deterrent than the probability of being caught, and this pattern is also found in the literature on tax compliance. The evidence that fear of detection is a deterrent is mixed. Mason and Calvin (1978) report that in their survey study the highest correlation with admitted evasion was the perceived probability of not being caught and many studies have found that evaders and participants in the underground economy perceive a lower probability of detection than others (e.g. Vogel 1974; Scott & Grasmick 1981; Grasmick & Scott 1982; Van Eck &

Kazemier 1988), although people generally overestimate the chance of being audited. Using IRS records from 1969, Dubin and Wilde (1988) also found that audits had a deterrent effect. Experimental studies have confirmed the importance of audit probability (e.g. Spicer & Thomas 1982; Webley & Halstead 1986). Two additional studies using TCMP data do not support this notion. Long (1980) used a classic deterrence econometric feedback model and TCMP data aggregated at the IRS district level. The estimated deterrent effect of audits found was demonstrated to be explainable by bias introduced through random sampling error. A second later study using individual level TCMP panel data showed little specific deterrent effect of an audit (Long & Schwartz 1987).

This raises the question of what influences people's perceptions of the probability of detection. To explore this issue, Klepper and Nagin (1989) presented individuals with a series of detailed scenarios about a hypothetical taxpayer. They found that age and itemisation of deductions were associated with perceiving lower probabilities of detection overall, but, more interestingly, perceived probabilities of detection varied according to the nature of the specific declaration made. So, for example, detection was seen as less likely for income not subject to third-party reporting and more likely if tax was evaded on a large proportion of an item (e.g. a charitable deduction).

Although the evidence that heavier penalties produce more compliance than lighter penalties is limited, it is undoubtedly the case that fines and other punishments are, to a certain extent, deterrents. Some researchers have argued that above a certain threshold of probability of detection a mild penalty is as effective a deterrent as a heavy one (see Friedland 1982), though Jackson and Jones (1985) found that when the probability of detection was low (less than 4%) people were sensitive to the size of the penalty. Witte and Woodbury (1985) found that there was a relationship between severity of sanctions and compliance but only for a specific group of taxpayers (those who had high incomes and were self-employed). This suggests that we need to know much more about individual differences in the personal consequences of penalties and how those penalties are perceived. Klepper and Nagin (1989) argue that the reason researchers (including themselves) have found no evidence that the severity of a penalty matters is that the personal costs of even mild penalties are heavy.

Given the somewhat mixed nature of the evidence it is perhaps surprising that the classic model has been so widely used. Our guess is that it is its very simplicity that is appealing. As models use more realistic assumptions their predictions often become more ambiguous and, as Allingham and Sandmo (1972, 329) themselves point out, 'even a model as simple as the present one does not generate any simple result concerning the relationship between income and tax evasion' (it depends upon the relationship between relative risk aversion and income). But there is widespread recognition that tax evasion cannot just be treated as a simple gamble. Apart from anything else, given the current mild sanctions and low probability of detection, this kind of approach would predict that virtually everybody should be evading tax (Smith & Kinsey 1987); in other words we should not be asking 'why do people evade taxes?' but rather 'why do people pay them?' (Alm, McClelland & Schulze 1989).

So there have been a variety of extensions to the simple model. We will describe just two of them here; interactive (game-playing) models (Corchon 1984; Benjamini & Maital 1985) and those that use the idea of limited rationality (Kahneman & Tversky 1979, 1984; Jackson & Milliron 1986; Schadewald 1989).

The interactive models stem from a recognition that a taxpayer is not taking decisions in isolation and that there are other 'players' in the 'game'. The revenue authorities can clearly alter the probability of detection and the penalty rate. They can change these over time and make them different for different taxpayers. The behaviour of other taxpayers may also be relevant. Your reputation may suffer if you are caught evading in a population largely comprised of nonevaders but will be unaffected or may even rise if most people evade taxes.

In the Corchon model (described by Cowell 1990), the tax situation is treated as a two-person game involving the taxpayer and the authorities. The taxpayer has two choices; he can either comply or not comply. The authorities also have two choices; they can either investigate the taxpayer or not. Clearly there is no simple equilibrium in this model. If the taxpayer is complying it is best for the authorities not to waste money investigating but, if the authorities are known not to be investigating, it is best for the taxpayer not to comply. But there is an equilibrium if both parties use mixed strategies. In this situation the probability of evasion increases with the marginal cost of investigation and decreases with the size of the penalty for evasion (as the penalty gets less the probability of playing the 'investigate' move approaches 1). Surprisingly, if the game is repeated the expected tax evaded is zero.

This kind of approach may look very simplistic but there have been some interesting developments. The game between the taxpayer and the authorities is not a symmetrical one; the participants are emphatically not of equal status. And there are many taxpayers. So the authorities can maximise their returns by treating different groups of taxpayers differently. A particularly neat model of this type, by Greenberg (1984), is described by Cowell (1985). Here the assumption, as always, is that everyone would cheat if it was worth their while. Naturally the government cannot afford to investigate everyone but it can reduce evasion dramatically if it divides the population into three groups rather than auditing the whole population at the same overall level.

Group A (presumed honest) have a small probability of being investigated. Group B (known evaders) have, paradoxically, an even smaller probability of being investigated. The poor unfortunates in group C (incorrigible evaders) are always investigated. The population is told about the existence of these groups and also told that each year individuals will be shifted from group to group according to a simple rule. If they are in group A and are caught evading they are moved to group B. If they are in group B and are audited what happens depends on their behaviour. If they are found to be honest they are considered redeemed and moved back to group A. If they are found to be cheating they are consigned to group C. Once you are in group C you are stuck there. The equilibrium for this situation is that most people are in group B (none of whom cheat because of the dire consequences of being found out), none are in group C and the rest are in group A (all of whom cheat). The reason that the audit frequency for the known evaders in group B is lower than that of the presumed honest members of group A, which seems unfair and counter-intuitive, is that the cost of being found out in group B is so high (never being able to cheat again) that a low-audit probability is enough to enforce compliance. From the authorities' point of view the low-audit probability keeps more people in the non-evading group B. For the same overall number of audits, there is less evasion in this system than there would be if the authorities treated taxpayers as a homogeneous group and audited at a standard level.

More interesting for psychologists, of course, are those extensions to the model that take into account the behaviour of other taxpayers, since these involve social psychological variables like stigma, reputation, and social norms. This is done by making the utility of a person's evasion partly a function of the size of the underground economy (Benjamini & Maital 1985; Cowell 1990). As this increases, the stigma of evading declines and other costs of evading (such as discovering how to do it) also drop. The details of this model are quite technical but suffice it to say that it has multiple stable equilibria. In a homogeneous population everybody either evades or is completely honest; more realistically, in a heterogeneous population members of certain groups will generally evade whilst members of others will be generally honest. Cowell (1990) suggests that this implies that the decision about evasion is a two-stage process; first a person decides whether to be honest or not and then proceeds to the fine calculations of how much to evade. Similarly Carroll (1987) describes the evasion decision as involving different strategies (such as how to evade).

Treating decisions as a two-stage process is also found in those approaches that posit limitations to rationality. The best known of these is Kahneman and Tversky's (1979, 1984) prospect theory, which was developed to overcome some problems in standard utility theory. They have argued that people make choices in two stages. In the first stage, the problem-editing phase, the individual reformulates options so that the subsequent choice is simplified. This editing consists of operations that transform the probabilities and outcomes such as simplification (e.g. rounding a probability of 0.49 to 0.50) and segregation (decomposing a choice into a riskless component and a risky choice). An important part of this process is the framing of outcomes (prospects) as gains and losses relative to some reference point, rather than as final states of wealth or utility. In the second phase, the evaluation phase, the individual evaluates each of the edited prospects and chooses the prospect with the highest value. In this stage the individual will use a utility function that is convex for losses, concave for gains, and steeper for losses than for gains. This implies that when sure gains are involved individuals will tend to avoid risks, whereas they will be willing to take risks to avoid sure losses. It also implies that people will take different decisions depending on how problems are framed.

A much cited example of this is given by Tversky and Kahneman (1981). Subjects are asked to imagine that the United States is threatened with an unusual disease that is expected to kill 600 people. A choice has to be made between two interventions. The first of these gives a certain outcome; 200 people will live and 400 will die. The second is risky; there is a one in three chance that 600 will live (no people will die) and a two in three chance that no people will live (600 will die). Which option do most people choose? This depends on how the problem is framed. If the situation is presented as a gain (e.g. 200 people will be saved versus a one in three chance of 600 being saved) most respondents go for the certain option. Conversely if it is presented as a loss (400 people will die) the risky choice is most popular.

The relevance of this to tax evasion has been noted by a number of researchers (Jackson & Milliron 1986; Schadewald 1989) and is discussed in some detail by Smith and Kinsey (1987). They point to several facts that implicate framing in tax decisions. For instance, an analysis of focus group discussions suggests that tax that has to be paid has greater utility than tax that is already withheld. It is also the case that a majority of taxpayers in the United States seem to prefer having more withheld than is strictly necessary. This implies that, in a system where tax is withheld by the authorities, individuals who expect a refund and perceive this as a gain should avoid the risks associated with evasion. On the other hand, those expecting to pay yet more tax (a certain loss) should be more likely to take the risky alternative and evade tax.

In fact, the evidence that prospect theory works in the tax domain is somewhat equivocal (the relevant literature is discussed in more detail in chapter 4). Leaving that on one side, it is worth noting that all the models described in this section share the assumption that the tax evader is simply greedy. They may differ on what goes into the utility function, the shape of that function or how the decision is reached but there is no dispute about underlying motivation. The models discussed in the next section are rather more varied.

1.3   Why do people evade taxes? Social psychological views

A surprisingly large number of sociological and social psychological theories of tax evasion have been proposed. We will not provide an exhaustive account here (for this see Kinsey 1986, or Hessing, Kinsey, Elffers & Weigel 1988). Instead we will be selective and discuss a few of the more interesting attempts, paying particular attention to those which seem to us genuinely to add to our understanding.

At the outset it is worth making a distinction between two kinds of theories. The first are integrative models of the taxpaying process, based on a wide knowledge of the literature and designed to introduce some new ideas. These are sometimes referred to as theories but are better seen as frameworks (and are sometimes so named by their authors) within which data about taxpaying and evasion can be organised. Good examples would be the models of Lewis (1982), Groenland and Van Veldhoven (1983), and Smith and Kinsey (1987). Some of the models one finds in the literature are essentially conceptual maps and are not really suitable for empirical testing. At their best they give us a feel for the crucial variables involved in evasion and how they might interrelate. At their worst they are reminiscent of the information-processing models of consumer behaviour found in marketing texts, with a multitude of little boxes connected by arrows bold and dotted. The disquieting thought here is that an arrow more or less would make little difference. The second kind are fairly straightforward applications of a social psychological theory to tax evasion (e.g. Kaplan, Reckers & Reynolds 1986). These sometimes suffer from being somewhat outdated. This distinction is not a hard and fast one, of course, and some of the frameworks have chunks of standard social psychology embedded in them. But it is a reasonable characterisation of the theories that are encountered.

We will begin with the broadest of the frameworks and then narrow down to the straightforward applications. We will end with our own approach, which we see (understandably enough) as an ideal blend; properly embedded in the tax context, genuinely social psychological and testable.

1.3.1   *Lewis (1982): Individuals and authorities*
In his book *The psychology of taxation*, Lewis (1982) reviewed the whole gamut of research into taxation and drew insights from a variety of disciplines. He was particularly concerned to fuse psychology and economics,

an enterprise that has latterly been extremely productive (see Cullis & Lewis 1985; Lewis & Cullis 1988). He put forward two models: one which brings together the concerns of the individual and the concerns of the authorities, the other which focuses on the relationship between tax attitudes and tax behaviour.

The first is a conceptual map. As far as the authorities are concerned, three factors are seen as important: the government's fiscal policy and the tax-enforcement policy (which affect each other) and the policy makers' assumptions about taxpayers. These assumptions are affected by the tax-enforcement structure and themselves weakly influence fiscal policy. The tax-enforcement structure partly determines the amount of evasion, which itself affects policy makers' assumptions. On the individual side another three factors are described. These are fiscal attitudes and perceptions (which include the individual's support for government policies, perceptions of the tax system and burden, feelings of alienation and inequity), perceptions of enforcement and opportunity, and characteristics of the taxpayers (demographics and personality traits). These all interact to affect the decision as to whether to evade tax or not.

The two sides (governmental and individual) also affect each other. Fiscal attitudes and perceptions are partly a result of actual government policy, and actual enforcement structure also affects perceived opportunities for evasion (though the evidence is that most people have little idea of the real chance of being detected). Conversely, the attitudes and perceptions of taxpayers feed into fiscal and enforcement policy. This gives us an idea of the kinds of variables that are important but comes up sharply against a general problem in economic psychology, that is, how to link the individual and the aggregate levels of analysis. We can see that the tax-enforcement structure will be linked in some way with people's views as to whether they can evade and get away with it. But the nature of the link is not specified. In the UK, for instance, we would guess that people's estimates of the chance of successfully evading are influenced more by the media's coverage of cases where well-known figures are prosecuted for evasion than by actual changes in auditing procedures. Furthermore, we are fairly sure that that is what the Inland Revenue believe. For each variable we need more detail on how decisions (whether individual or governmental) are reached. Lewis' second model, on the relationship between tax attitudes and tax behaviour provides this detail.

This is essentially Fishbein and Ajzen's (1975) theory of reasoned action (see also Ajzen & Fishbein 1980), applied to the tax field with the addition of a set of pertinent exogenous variables (in Fishbein and Ajzen's version behavioural intention is seen as a function of two, and only two, variables: the person's attitude to the behaviour and the subjective norm). The exogenous variables include demographic variables, attitudes towards the 'targets' of evasion (the government, tax inspectors), and personality traits. These are seen as factors that will influence the relative importance of the attitudinal and normative components and feed into the other important variables in the Fishbein and Ajzen equation. Fishbein and Ajzen's theory has undoubted predictive power but its descriptive validity is uncertain (Van der Pligt & Eiser 1984). It is, in essence, a subjective expected utility model and these are not good descriptions of the way people actually make decisions (Lea, Tarpy & Webley 1987). Lewis himself points out the difficulty of actually testing it when a behaviour is private and illegal; as he says (1982, 174) 'without information about behavioural intentions or behaviour itself, the principal weapon of this approach, its predictive capacity, can fire only blanks'.

1.3.2   Smith and Kinsey (1987): Tax decisions in a social context

In outlining their approach Smith and Kinsey make a number of useful points. First, most researchers have seen evasion as a deviation from a normal or nonproblematic state of compliance. This assumption may be plausible for employees in countries like the UK but under some tax regimes (the self-employed in the UK, all taxpayers in the US and the Netherlands) compliance itself has considerable costs (Sandford 1973; Sandford, Godwin, Hardwick & Butterworth 1981; Slemrod & Sorum 1984). Swingen and Long (1988a) report that 29% of 1987 tax returns were completed by paid preparers. This is particularly interesting as Long (1989) found that, after TRA 86, professional tax preparers in their study faced up to half an hour more time, saw an increase of preparation fees of about 20%, and reported a 19% overall increase in the volume of prepared returns. So we need to understand what factors motivate compliance as much as what factors motivate evasion. Second, many analyses of evasion focus on the preferences and intentions of taxpayers and largely ignore the social context. Not only do the marked differences in opportunities need to be taken into account but also social networks and group processes generally. Third and finally, almost all past research has assumed that noncompliance is the result of a conscious and deliberate decision by taxpayers. We know that many people make mistakes on their tax forms: James, Lewis, and Allison (1987) report that around 80% of taxpaying pensioners in the UK make errors in their tax forms, and Swingen and Long (1988b) say that between 2.9% and 10.8% of taxpayer prepared returns in the US have mathematical and clerical errors that are obvious from a superficial examination. More importantly, in many situations compliance may simply be the result of inertia. In addition, people probably do not take a single decision to evade. It is more likely that, through a series of actions such as keeping good records or guesstimating expenses, they end up complying (or not).

Smith and Kinsey differentiate between the process and the content of decision making. They feel that most research to date has concentrated on accounting for the latter, specifically the decision to cheat, and has ignored the decision process. They present a flow chart of this which shows what factors shift people from their habitual behaviour to consciously taking a decision and forming intentions. Generally speaking, aspects of the social context such as tax reform, changes in the economy, and changes in pay will make taxes more salient. Then people will move through three stages; diagnostic (in which the situation is defined), action (in which intentions are formed), and implementation (in which they decide how to carry out intentions). At any point individuals may return to their habitual response; they may decide that the costs of taking a decision are not worth the effort or they may form an intention but not act on it (if, for example, there is no opportunity to realise it).

As far as content is concerned, people are seen as weighing four clusters of factors in forming intentions: material consequences, normative expectations, socio-legal attitudes and expressive factors. This is done in prospect-theory terms; that is, decisions are framed in terms of gains and losses from some initial reference point. Material consequences are the province of economic models and also of Fishbein and Ajzen's (1975) theory of reasoned action (which also incorporates the idea of normative expectations). We have already encountered these aspects in Lewis' (1982) model. None the less Smith and Kinsey add to our understanding in two ways. They introduce celerity (the promptness with which consequences occur) as a relevant variable and point out that the private nature of taxpaying sets limits on norm acquisition. Celerity is easy to add to economic models, ties in with psychological research, and fits with common sense; a long delay between crime and punishment will lessen the deterrent effect of the latter. As for the private nature of taxpaying, it is probably only in those groups which favour evasion where conversations about the behaviour are usual. If individuals fear informal sanctions for evasion they only have to keep quiet.

Socio-legal opinions and expressive factors are less often included in models. Two kinds of opinions are considered; about the goals that are dependent on taxes (i.e. government spending) and about the tax system itself. Since many people do not recognise the link between taxation and government expenditure (the so-called 'fiscal connection', Lewis 1982), Smith and Kinsey believe that attitudes towards goals have indirect effects that work through attitudes to the system itself. But these too only have indirect effects on intentions through the material consequences. Expressive factors (perhaps better called 'psychic costs'), on the other hand, have a direct effect. These are simply the subjective costs and benefits involved with taxpaying, such as the frustration involved in completing tax forms.

This framework, of which only the sketchiest outline has been given here, has the merit of providing an overall picture of the taxpaying process whilst at the same time setting out some testable hypotheses.

1.3.3   Groenland and Van Veldhoden (1983): Personality and situational characteristics as determinants of evasion

Groenland and Van Veldhoven put forward a tentative framework which fused *ad hoc* approaches with attitude-behaviour models. Individual differences (in this case 'locus of control') and situational characteristics interact to affect attitude towards (and knowledge of) the tax system, which in turn affects the disposition to evade. These dispositions and situational characteristics then have direct effects on actual behaviour. Three different kinds of situational characteristics are discussed, opportunity, socio-economic factors, and tax system. These are all seen as having the potential directly and indirectly to affect evasion. Thus the particular configuration of the tax system will provide opportunities for evasion for certain groups and influence attitudes towards it.

Unlike the Lewis (1982) and Smith and Kinsey (1987) frameworks, this somewhat simpler approach has been empirically tested in Holland (by Groenland and Van Veldhoven themselves) and in Sweden (Wärneryd 1980). The results could be described as providing some support for the model (Hessing, Kinsey, Elffers & Weigel 1988) but, since only simple regression analysis was used, really tell us only that certain variables do predict fiscal knowledge, dispositions, and evasion. That the results are comparable across two countries with rather different economic and tax systems suggests the variables are 'good' ones but leaves open the question of causal structure.

1.3.4   Vogel (1974): A social psychological typology of taxpayers

Based on a survey of Swedish taxpayers, Vogel (1974) presents a theoretical framework and, more interestingly, a typology of taxpayers. In the framework, three objective factors are seen as having direct and indirect effects on tax opinions and evasion. These are the individual's exchange relationship with the government (tax burden minus government services received), social orientation (not defined theoretically but measured in terms of social class, party membership, etc.), and opportunities for evasion. These objective factors have indirect effects on evasion through their effect on tax attitudes and perceived opportunities. Knowing others who evade tax is also included as an important factor. As with Groenland and Van Veldhoven, the associated empirical work does fit the model, but again this tells us only that the variables that are identified are important.

The typology is based on Kelman's (1965) distinction between compliance, identification, and internalisation. Compliance is conforming outwardly to what an authority requires. So you pay taxes because you will suffer if you do not and not because you feel it is morally right to do so. Identification involves a change in beliefs in order to be like a person you admire. If your friends approve of tax evasion you will tend to do it. Internalisation involves a genuine change of beliefs in which ideas are integrated into a person's value system. Here the sanction feared is guilt.

Vogel combines Kelman's distinctions with two types of tax behaviour (cheating and compliance) to give six categories of individual adaption to the tax system. Starting from the moral high ground we have the conformist internalisers. They will pay taxes in full because they are morally committed taxpayers. The opposite side of the coin is the deviant internaliser, who is a tax protester rather than a cheater. Those people in the UK who intend not to pay the poll tax on ideological grounds would be a good example. Conformist identifiers and deviant identifiers will pay taxes (or not) because of the norms of their reference group. They fear the stigma of being different, which may involve informal sanctions like ridicule or ostracism. Conformist compliers pay because they fear punishment whereas deviant compliers evade because the chances of being caught and punished are low.

Vogel tried to fit his respondents into these categories on the basis of their self-reports of behaviour and their perceptions of the tax system and tax regulations. This was not completely successful because of the difficulty of devising clear assignment rules but the typology none the less provides an interesting insight into individual differences in this area.

1.3.5   An attribution approach to tax evasion

Attribution theory is concerned with how people make sense of their social world by attributing causes to one thing or another. To simplify Heider (1958), people do things because they have to (environmental cause) or because they want to (internal cause). So in interviewing for a job that requires outgoing people, an interviewer would probably attribute a candidate's quiet introverted behaviour to his or her personality (internal cause) but would be uncertain of how to explain extroverted behaviour as the situation requires this.

This basic approach has been elaborated and extended by Jones and Davis (1965) and Kelley (1967), applied to our understanding of our own behaviour and, more recently, to a variety of economic phenomena (e.g. Smith & Hunt 1978; Van Raaij 1985). Kaplan, Reckers, and Reynolds (1986) and Hite (1987) have applied it to tax evasion.

Kaplan, Reckers, and Reynolds claim that several principles in attribution theory may be useful in formulating hypotheses about tax evasion and base their discussion on the work of Kelley (1967). Kelley identified three attribution rules which are used when we have information from many observations: distinctiveness, consensus, and consistency. Briefly, one will attribute the cause of an impression to personal character if other individuals are perceived differently (distinctiveness), if others share the same impression (consensus), and if continued observation of the person confirms the impression (consistency). Thus, if many people evade tax, the fact that a particular individual is noncompliant tells you little about him, and Kaplan, Reckers, and Reynolds claim that, in this case, the individual would be seen as less responsible and therefore a lesser punishment is appropriate. Similarly, if individuals cheated only on their taxes and in no other context, this would lead to an attribution to the tax situation (based on its 'distinctiveness'). Their study provided only limited support for their predictions. For example, the distinctiveness prediction 'worked' but, contrary to their expectation, when tax evasion was uncommon people believed that a lower amount of punishment was appropriate.

Hite (1987) based her study on a different aspect of attribution research, that of actor-observer differences (Watson, 1982). It is a fairly consistent finding that, across a variety of domains, actors tend to explain their own behaviour by reference to aspects of the situation whereas they explain the behaviour of others in dispositional terms. Applied to evasion, this implies that individuals will see their own tax cheating as the result of, say, high tax rates, but the cheating of others as the result of poor morals. Hite's study provides some evidence for this, in that those subjects who had to assume they were an individual portrayed in a scenario did indeed explain 'their' behaviour differently from those who had to assume the main character was somebody else.

Our feeling about both of these studies is that they are far too naive. Both Kaplan *et al.* and Hite show little awareness of critical work on attribution theory (see Antaki 1981; Jaspars, Hewstone & Fincham 1983) and Kaplan, Reckers, and Reynolds seem unfamiliar with the related work on attribution of responsibility (Fincham & Jaspars 1980). The lay understanding of taxation and evasion is an interesting topic but is probably best pursued along other lines.

1.3.6   *Weigel, Hessing, and Elffers (1987): Tax evasion as defective behaviour within a social dilemma*

It is a commonplace that every behaviour is simultaneously personal and situational. But theories that emphasise the interactive influence of social and psychological variables are rare. Weigel, Hessing, and Elffers' approach, on which our work is based, is one such theory. Essentially this is derived from Jessor, Graves, Hansen, and Jessor's (1968) general theory of deviance.

The core of this approach is that evading taxes can be seen as a defective act within a social dilemma. A social dilemma (commons tragedy or social trap are alternative names) is characterised by two features. First, individuals get a better outcome if they make a defective choice rather than a cooperative one. Second, everybody is worse off if all make a defective choice. The classic example is an open common where each individual benefits if he or she alone grazes extra animals, but if everybody does this the carrying capacity of the common is reduced by overgrazing and everybody suffers (Hardin 1968). The tax system confronts people with a choice between cooperative behaviour (paying taxes in full) or defective behaviour (evading some or all taxes). Particular individuals would be better off if they paid less tax but the whole system would break down if too many people evaded. The analogy is not perfect, of course, since people have different opportunities and the penalty system is differentially applied. But it is an appropriate overall characterisation.

Conceiving the taxpayer as being part of a social dilemma immediately directs attention to the motivational orientation of individuals as this has been a long-term focus of social dilemma research (see Liebrand 1984; Johnson & Norem-Hebeisen 1979). Are they cooperative, individualistic or competitive? But individual differences, though an important part of the model, are only part of it. The framework (presented in Figure 1.1) specifies two kinds of variables: instigations and constraints. These variables are found both in the individual and the situation he is confronted with. We will deal with instigations first. Financial strain, the amount of tax owed after withholding, is a situational variable. This should produce more evasion. But not all people who are under financial strain evade tax. This will depend on whether this strain induces feelings of unfairness in the individual (personal strain). As in this instance, each situational variable is paired with one in the individual. So social norms, such as those supposedly prevalent in contemporary Britain, which stress wealth as a measure of status have their parallel in personal orientations which are self-serving rather than altruistic.

We use the concepts of instigations and constraints in a special way. People might indeed see 'constraints' and 'instigations' just as each other's mirror images. We try to distinguish them in the following way. Instigations have their place in an early stage of the psychological process of contemplating tax evasion. Constraints are thought to come into play at a later stage, namely after instigations have exerted their influence. So, after feeling instigated to evade tax, people start to think about the constraints. They will feel either worried when the constraints are perceived to be severe, or reassured when the constraints are seen to be lacking.

Constraints show the same pattern. Three sets of parallel variables are described. Opportunity to evade is a social factor. If you are often paid in cash or are self-employed with lots of deduction possibilities you objectively have a

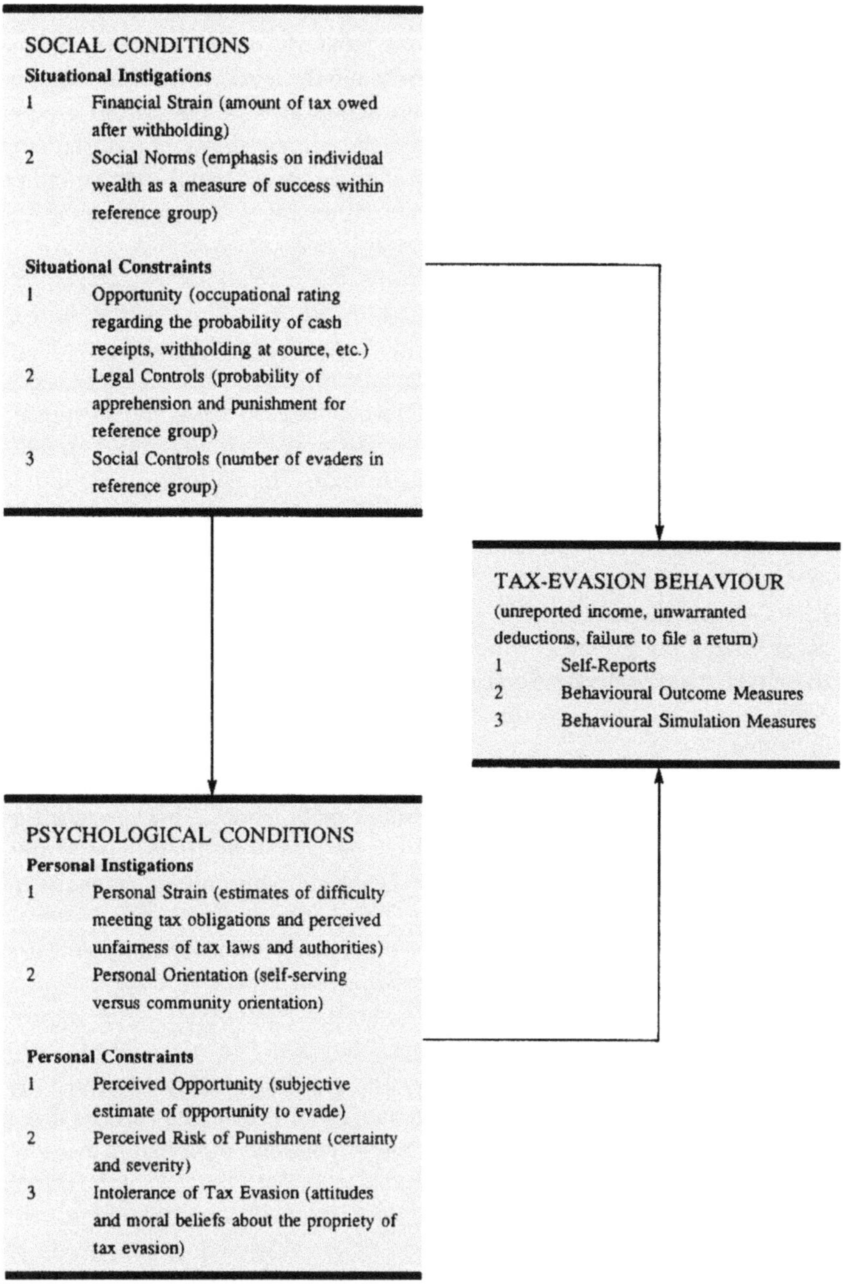

SOCIAL CONDITIONS

Situational Instigations

1   Financial Strain (amount of tax owed after withholding)
2   Social Norms (emphasis on individual wealth as a measure of success within reference group)

Situational Constraints

1   Opportunity (occupational rating regarding the probability of cash receipts, withholding at source, etc.)
2   Legal Controls (probability of apprehension and punishment for reference group)
3   Social Controls (number of evaders in reference group)

TAX-EVASION BEHAVIOUR

(unreported income, unwarranted deductions, failure to file a return)

1   Self-Reports
2   Behavioural Outcome Measures
3   Behavioural Simulation Measures

PSYCHOLOGICAL CONDITIONS

Personal Instigations

1   Personal Strain (estimates of difficulty meeting tax obligations and perceived unfairness of tax laws and authorities)
2   Personal Orientation (self-serving versus community orientation)

Personal Constraints

1   Perceived Opportunity (subjective estimate of opportunity to evade)
2   Perceived Risk of Punishment (certainty and severity)
3   Intolerance of Tax Evasion (attitudes and moral beliefs about the propriety of tax evasion)

Figure 1.1   A social psychological model of individual income tax-evasion behaviour (adapted from Weigel, Hessing, and Elffers 1987, 229). Examples of the variables in the model are included in brackets.

great opportunity to evade. But perceived opportunity depends upon a subjective estimate of the evasion options. Similarly, differences in the actual legal controls on evasion (audit frequency and the level of punishment) may account for variations in evasion rates across groups, but within groups individuals will take decisions based on the perceived risk of punishment. Lastly, social controls (approval and disapproval) will depend on the number of tax evaders in an individual's reference group and will be mediated by the development of associated attitudes towards evasion.

We would like to emphasise two features of the relationship between the social and psychological halves of the framework. First, the variables mirror each other – there is an objective social condition and a parallel subjective psychological condition. Second, and because of this, the framework provides a basis for examining the role of individual attributes in mediating the impact of social conditions. A further point worth making is that the variables proposed are seen as sufficient to explain evasion. This may seem odd, in that other models often include demographic variables, like sex, age, and social class, that consistently predict evasion. But it is rare indeed to come across explanations of why such demographics are relevant and their inclusion seems to be more a matter of measurement convenience. From our perspective these excluded variables are mediated through one or more of those which are included. So occupational status, age, sex, and income are crude approximations of the situational opportunities available to an individual.

In their more general approach to social dilemmas, Hessing and Elffers (1985) have produced a social-orientation meta-model. This specifies the situations under which central attitudes, peripheral attitudes, and norms predict behaviour in a social dilemma. Two distinctions are made: between public and private acts and between situations where the behaviour concerns self–other allocations and those where it does not. The essential points are that norms will have an influence on behaviour only if that behaviour is public and visible and that central attitudes (i.e. motivational orientations) will be much more relevant with private behaviour. The relevance of this to tax evasion is that, although evasion itself is a private act, it is often measured in a public way (through self-report). So this predicts that self-reported evasion may be predicted by rather different variables than actual evasion.

So far this model has stood up reasonably well. With the help of the Dutch Ministry of Finance, Elffers, Weigel, and Hessing (1987) were able to measure self-reported behaviour and officially documented behaviour of a group of taxpayers (more details of the method are given in chapter 2). Remarkably there was a negligible correlation between the two dependent measures. The personal constraint measures (fear of punishment, social controls, and attitudes towards underreporting income and making false deductions) were correlated with self-reported behaviour but unrelated to documented behaviour. Conversely, personal instigation measures (dissatisfaction with the tax authorities, motivational orientation variables like competitiveness, alienation, and tolerance of deviance) were correlated with documented behaviour but not self-reported behaviour. This pattern of results was partially supported in our early experimental studies (see chapter 3). These results certainly support the view that taxpaying may be seen as a social dilemma but leave open the question of how valid the whole framework is. However, on the analogous social dilemma of social security fraud they recently published a study in which the complete model was tested and successfully supported by the data (Robben, Elffers & Verlind 1989).

1.4 The wider social context: The importance of norms, cultural rules, and differences in tax systems

Taxes are to be found everywhere. Tax evasion is similarly ubiquitous. This is both a problem and an opportunity. As citizens from all around the world have taken part, it is a behaviour that can be found in a huge variety of cultural and legal settings. It therefore provides social scientists with a unique opportunity to study an individual behaviour with a high societal relevance across a range of cultures. It also means that researchers can try out different theoretical approaches from different disciplines. Through cross-national comparisons, it encourages us to look for both explanations that are generally valid and explanations that explain differences between different cultures and so shed light on the relationship between an individual and his or her society.

The reader will have noticed, however, that the models described above are generally rather individualistic. Even those that can be described as social psychological do not operate at a societal level. To understand evasion we really do need to know something about the history and current functioning of tax systems in different countries as well as what Schmölders (1970) calls the tax mentality of their citizens.

At the most basic level there are interesting semantic differences in the language used to describe taxes. The Dutch for tax is *belasting*, which also means load and so has the connotations of a burden. This is found in the Latin languages (*impôt, imposto, impuesto*; cognate with the English 'imposition') as well. But in German *Steuer* means support and the Scandinavian *skat* denotes a treasure or hoard (Schmölders 1970).

These linguistic differences, though interesting, are probably not very significant (there is no evidence that *skattefritt* in Scandinavia is less than *la fraude fiscale* in France). History is more important. The UK, which first introduced income tax in 1799 to help pay for the Napoleonic wars, rapidly developed an effective structure to administer it. The various schedules, which deal with income from particular sources, were introduced in 1803 and are, with slight modifications, still operating today. The 'Pay As You Earn' system, which has been an effective counter to evasion, was introduced under the impetus of the second world war. Before the war less than a fifth of the working population paid income tax but by 1948 this had increased to two-thirds and now it is more than 90% (Rose & Karran 1987). So for a long time the population have been used to paying income tax. By way of contrast, the tax system in operation in Spain in the 1960s was described as 'primitive' by Schmölders (1970). It had a predominance of indirect taxes, was generally regressive and was widely regarded as unfair. The reform of 1977 brought in a progressive system with far more revenue being collected in the form of income tax. In 1976 just under one and a third million people made tax returns. This grew to almost 3 million in 1978 and over 6 million in 1980. Despite this modernisation of the system the belief that it is unfair has persisted, probably because more people are aware of paying tax (direct taxation is more visible than indirect taxation) and because the government is seen as wasting money (Alvira Martin & Garcia Lopez 1984).

A different kind of historical factor is implicated in the Italian case. It has been claimed (Haycraft 1985) that, because for centuries large parts of Italy were ruled by foreigners, citizens never developed a trusting relationship with their government and always preferred to spend money on their friends and relatives than on any remote authority. The payment of taxes was seen not as a duty but as something to be avoided if at all possible. Haycraft claims that this attitude persists today and that many ancient sayings that epitomise it (such as 'he who robs the king does no sin') are still quoted with approval.

Historical factors give us some insight into the tax mentality of different countries. But current practices are probably the most significant. We are obviously not going to provide a guide to tax systems around the world, or even around Europe (for this see Platt 1980, 1982). But we will say something about the most important differences in tax systems and give actual details on the systems in the Netherlands, the UK, and the US.

Before we do this we need to explain what a tax is. This is not, as you might think, self-evident; as Messere and Owens (1987) say, 'taxes are difficult both to define and identify'. The OECD (Organisation for Economic Cooperation and Development) defines a tax as 'compulsory, unrequited payments to general government'. Thus, although many British people would not think of their National Insurance payments as a tax, under this definition they are. They are compulsory and do not take into account factors which a genuine insurance scheme would include. Dutch health insurance is compulsory up to a certain income and optional thereafter. So, by the OECD definition, contributions below the ceiling are taxes and those above it are not.

Table 1.1. *Receipts from taxes as a percentage of GDP in 1983*

	Total taxes	Income tax	Social security
Sweden	50	20	13
Netherlands	47	10	17
Norway	47	12	10
Denmark	46	24	2
Belgium	45	16	13
France	45	6	18
Austria	41	9	12
Italy	41	11	13
Ireland	39	12	6
UK	38	10	6
Germany	37	11	13
Greece	33	4	10
US	30	11	8
Japan	28	7	7
Spain	27	6	11

Source: Messere and Owens (1987), Table 2

Taxes are usually categorised as direct (income) or indirect (consumption) (Allan 1971). Direct taxes are more visible to the taxpayer (income tax, poll tax, capital transfer tax) whereas indirect taxes are often less visible and collected by an intermediary. VAT and excise duty are good examples. In this book we are concerned only with direct taxes. The rate structure of a tax is usually described as being progressive, proportional, or regressive. Taxes that take an increasing proportion of income as it rises are progressive, those that take a constant proportion are proportional, and those that take a decreasing proportion are regressive. The UK government's community charge (or poll tax) is clearly regressive whereas the income-tax system is roughly progressive.

The most important differences between tax systems concern the overall level of taxation, the tax structure, and the marginal tax rates. The overall level of taxation can be expressed as tax revenue as a percentage of GDP. Table 1.1 gives this information for some selected countries. From this table it can be seen that the tax and social-security burden varies considerably from one country to the next. Generally the countries with the highest per capita GDP have the heaviest burden, but there are important exceptions, like the US and Japan. Four southern European countries (France, Italy, Spain, and Greece) share certain characteristics. They have large numbers of people who are self-employed or who work in agriculture, there is a relaxed attitude to smoking and drinking, and a large chunk of revenue comes from social security rather than income tax. It is less easy to generalise about

Table 1.2. *Marginal tax
rates on average wages in
1986 (include social security
contributions) (%)*

Belgium	63
Germany	63
Denmark	62
Netherlands	62
Sweden	62
Ireland	60
Norway	60
Italy	58
Austria	54
Spain	53
France	51
UK	44
US	41
Greece	40
Japan	32

Source: Hagemann, Jones & Montador (1988), Table 6

Scandinavia and the Low Countries, which have the highest tax ratio. These
countries generally have high marginal tax rates too. The contrast in
marginal rates is quite remarkable. Clearly the financial incentive to evade
income tax is stronger in the Netherlands or Sweden than in Britain or Japan.

This broad picture makes it clear that the incentives, opportunities and
meaning of evasion to individuals differ between countries. A more detailed
consideration of particular tax systems hammers this message home. We will
spare the reader an exhaustive account of the minutiae of English, American,
and Dutch tax law but we will briefly describe some of the more salient
characteristics. There are three reasons for doing this. First, people are a little
egocentric about tax systems and assume that others function like their own.
Second, and related to this, to understand the basis for the research on
withholding/overpayment described in chapter 4 requires an understanding
of pay-as-you-go systems (subtly different from the British PAYE). Third, as
our experiments were carried out in Holland and Britain information about
the system that the participants were familiar with is helpful. For instance, in
the UK to date, married couples have generally made joint returns signed by
the husband, which means that wives usually have little or no experience of
tax forms.

The UK's PAYE procedure is unique, though a similar system operates in

Ireland (it was widely, if unfairly, called Pay ALL You Earn when first introduced). It is able to withhold tax very accurately and requires little cooperation from taxpayers – most of the necessary paperwork is done by employers and the Inland Revenue. The basic difference between it and the American and Dutch system is that it is cumulative; that is, a taxpayer's pay and allowances are accumulated through the year and the amount withheld in a particular month is dependent on the income received up to that month. This means that the right tax is withheld throughout the year and rebates can be made during the year, rather than at the end of it. With the American and Dutch systems earnings are taxed each month as though they were one-twelfth of earnings during the year. So only if earnings are constant is the right amount withheld. If income drops to zero in a particular month no tax is paid, whereas under PAYE a refund is paid.

One notable feature of the British system in practice is that the taxpayer does not have to make an annual tax return. After an individual has given the Inland Revenue information about personal circumstances a new return is needed only if circumstances change. Barr, James, and Prest (1977) report that, in most cases, tax returns are completed about once every five years. In contrast, in the US and Holland tax returns have to be made annually and in most cases an end-of-year adjustment is required. In the US, 73% of the 1988 returns had refunds (SOI Bulletin, IRS publication 1989).

Another interesting contrast is that in the USA and Holland the individual can claim a variety of deductions, whereas for employees in the UK very few expenditures can be deducted. To give a concrete and personal example, PW claims only for his subscription to the British Psychology Society whereas DJH claims for many forms of expenditure such as scientific books and journals, the running costs of a study room at home (i.e. a fraction of the rent and part of the bills for electricity, telephone and cleaning), and gifts. Examples of common personal deductions allowed in the US are home-mortgage interest and state income taxes. The recent tax reforms in the US and the Netherlands have, however, limited the deductions severely, excluding many alternatives or limiting claims to amounts above thresholds which exceed most ordinary taxpayers' expenses.

One final feature is the differences in tax bands, or tax *brackets* as they are called in the US. In the UK there are now only two: the first 20,700 pounds of taxable income is taxed at 25% and anything above this is taxed at 40%. In the Dutch case there are currently tax bands of 35.75%, 50%, and 60%. The Tax Reform Act of 1986 in the US reduced the number of individual tax bands to two (15% and 28%), plus a surtax band of 33% for certain high-income individuals.

A detailed knowledge of tax structure, tax rates and tax revenue as a percentage of Gross National Product, etc. does not, of course, tell us anything about how taxpayers feel about their particular system. For this we need cross-national studies of tax attitudes and the like and for this we shall rely on Schmölder's (1959, 1970) pioneering work into fiscal psychology. With colleagues, he carried out a series of large-scale survey studies of tax enforcement techniques and 'tax mentality' in the UK, France, Germany, Spain, and Italy. They found a marked contrast between the UK and Germany and the other three countries. The French, Italian, and Spanish systems were similar to each other and were characterised as ineffectual and expensive. In the business sector, 'book-keeping is unreliable, auditing is incompetent, cooperation with the tax office is practically nonexistent and law enforcement, on the other hand, minimal . . . even the sales figures delivered to the tax office are in most cases quite unreliable' (Schmölders, 1970, 301). The tax mentality in these countries is correspondingly poor and evading tax seen as quite legitimate. The German and British systems, by contrast, were both effective in meeting their allocative and distributional goals but in rather different ways. In Germany, relatively coercive enforcement techniques were used which led to high compliance costs, particularly for the self-employed. Consequently citizens were rather alienated, had negative tax attitudes, felt the system to be unfair but did generally pay their taxes properly (in Vogel's terms, they had not identified with the system and were simply compliant). In Britain, there was, apparently 'a frictionless functioning of the tax system', partly because of easy opportunities for avoidance by the self-employed.

This work, though extensive, is limited in two important ways. First, it is mainly concerned with the self-employed and second, it describes the picture twenty years ago. We simply do not have comparable surveys from the 1980s to draw on.

We said at the outset of this section that tax evasion provided researchers with a great opportunity. There is only one serious problem: measuring the behaviour is extremely difficult. It is to this that we now turn.

2 The problem of measurement

2.1 Introduction

Measurement problems constitute one of the most important roadblocks to the advancement of social science Blalock (1975, 359)

Roadblocks can be dismantled, driven round, or, if you drive fast enough, smashed through. Although the last solution makes for a more exciting story, here we have a more pedestrian aim: to analyse the nature of the block and suggest a partial solution.

The major problem facing research into tax evasion is undoubtedly how to measure it. This comprises two subproblems: what behaviour can be called tax evasion (discussed in chapter 1) and how can we determine whether or not it takes place? As a corollary there is the question of when exactly people can be said to be evading tax: is it the act of filing a return knowing it to be inaccurate (the legal view) or when they contemplate misrepresenting their financial position, something which may take place much earlier? People may collect receipts for expenditures that are not really deductible, ask to be paid in cash or draw up diabolical constructions to mislead the tax authorities (Carroll 1987). It is likely then that evasion is best understood not as a single act (the illegal declaration) but as a series of actions and decisions (see Smith & Kinsey, 1987). However, in an experiment there is the possibility of condensing the 'process of tax evading' into a single act or a couple of single acts, which are – more or less – easy to measure.

2.1.1 Sources of data

The differences found in the kind of theory devised by economists and psychologists are also found, although to a lesser extent, in the kind of measurement they have used. Economists have favoured the 'hardest' data they can get whereas psychologists have been content with a variety of 'softer' approaches based on self-report. Instead of using this rather evaluative 'hard/soft' categorisation we will distinguish between direct, personal measures (assessed at the individual level) and indirect, aggregated measures (assessed at an aggregate level). The latter kind of measurement is found mainly in macro-economic contexts and was briefly discussed in the previous chapter. It involves using indices such as the percentage of banknotes issued that are of large denominations or the divergence between income and expenditure estimates of GDP. Other sources of this kind of data also exist, such as the aggregated data reported by the tax authorities. Direct data, however, are generally derived from research using self-reports of individual taxpayers, or more rarely from official records. These self-reports may involve direct questioning ('Did you report your income fully this year?'), as well as more indirect measurement ('Do you have friends and relations who do not always state their income honestly?').

2.1.2   Indirect data
A variety of indirect methods has been used. In addition to these approaches already described (looking at money and discrepancies in the estimates of GDP), there is also the technique of examining labour-market participation rates. This rests on the assumption that some of the officially unemployed are in fact earning money. By contrasting the participation rates over time and between countries it is possible to produce estimates of the relative extent of the shadow economy (e.g. Contini 1981). In 1975, for example, the official participation rate in Italy was 35% whereas in the US and the UK it was 45%. Moreover, the Italian participation rate has been falling in the past few years.

Earlier we characterised all these indirect methods as providing 'guesstimates' about evasion. This may seem a little harsh, but consider a few facts. The estimates cover a very wide range: for 1976 in the US from 3.4% (Tanzi 1980) to 21.7% (Feige 1979); for Sweden in the late seventies from 0.5% to 17.2% (Frey & Weck 1987). Even if you look only at estimates produced using the same method the range is almost as large. So it is not possible to take them at their face value.

On a more theoretical level, the estimates depend on some strong assumptions which may be rather unrealistic. For instance, with the monetary method, there are assumptions about the stability of the demand for currency over time and about the equivalence of money velocity in the official and unofficial economy, both of which may not be justified. In addition, Frey and Weck (1987) point out that the estimates depend on which base year is chosen. If 1963 was used as the base instead of 1974, one method would then show a negative unofficial economy for the UK!

Perhaps most crucially, these indirect methods cannot be used to research the association of evasion with other interesting factors, in so far as these are characteristics of individuals. Of course it is possible to look at the effect on the extent of evasion in different countries of aggregate variables such as the burden of taxation, the length of the official working week and overall tax mentality (Frey & Weck 1987). Without reliable and comparable estimates, however, it is difficult to know what to make of such analyses.

2.1.3 Data from official files

Studies using direct, personal data derived from official files are rare but extremely interesting (Clotfelter 1983; Wallschutsky 1984; Slemrod 1985). Wallschutsky (1984) capitalised on the fact that the Australian authorities then published the names of convicted tax evaders. He compared relevant tax attitudes and opinions of a sample of the convicted group with a sample drawn from the electoral register. The measure of evasion here was actual conviction. But, as Wallschutsky himself noted, his general sample was probably contaminated by a large number of unconvicted evaders, which may account for the fact that few significant differences were found between the two groups. Drost and Jongman (1982) report – based on their study inside the office of a Dutch tax inspectorate – that 34% of the tax forms filed in 1974 were incorrect. Overall, 22% were defined as fraudulent returns. An interesting aspect of this study is the authors' claim that of these fraud cases only 3% were fined and only 0.003% were sanctioned in court. This means that of all tax returns filed in 1974, 0.0007% (i.e. 25 cases) were sentenced in court.

The other three studies all used information supplied by the US Internal Revenue Service. Clotfelter (1983) used data from the Taxpayer Compliance Measurement Program, which consists of very large samples of individual tax returns. Noncompliance was defined as the difference between reported income and the amount of income that the IRS auditors determined was due. Those who were overcompliant (in some cases taxpayers report too much income) were treated as honest. This measure of evasion is attractively simple but has a number of limitations. First, it assesses only those instances of evasion that can be detected by auditors. It is very difficult for auditors to discover certain forms of unreported income, such as income from moonlighting and cash-only businesses, and obviously there is no information on taxpayers who did not file returns. Second, there is no way of distinguishing between deliberate evasion and unintended errors. To get an overall estimate of evasion one can subtract the percentage of those overreporting (an indication of the expected rate of honest mistakes) from the percentage of those underreporting, but there is no way of doing anything comparable on an individual level. Third, the TCMP data has very limited information about personal variables and because the anonymity of the individuals in the sample precludes follow-up, it is not possible to explore the social and psychological factors associated with noncompliance.

Slemrod (1985) also used a stratified random sample of US tax returns but used a very different and ingenious measure of evasion. The model presented is quite complex but the basic idea is to draw inferences about unreported income from reported income. This rests on the observation that for most taxpayers tax liability is a step function of taxable income. The step length is 50 dollars. Slemrod's argument is that individuals evading income will tend to declare taxable income at the top of these 50 dollar brackets whereas honest individuals will be distributed evenly throughout the range.

Although clever, this method has a number of limitations. It is based entirely on declared income (i.e. those not filing returns are excluded) and operates at an aggregate rather than individual level. Consider Slemrod's evidence that older people evade less. Age is not given on tax returns so a proxy variable (the claiming of an age exemption) is used. However, the differences found were extremely small. Overall 19.5% of those claiming at least one age exemption are in the top $10 of the $50 brackets compared to 21.1% of those not claiming age exemptions. Again, individuals are anonymous, so more detailed psychological information is unobtainable.

Interestingly enough, economists (e.g. Baldry 1987) tend to regard these data as 'hard' and have more trust in them than in self-reports. Criminologists, on the other hand, generally stress the invalidity of official data on deviant behaviour (Walsh & Poole 1983). Instead of seeing criminal statistics as a reflection of the prevalence of criminal behaviour, they would be more likely to focus on the processes by which the statistics are generated. For most offences it is clear that official records underestimate the extent of the problem and evasion is probably no exception to this rule. This underestimation is often a result of victims not reporting crime but it may also be because the offence is overlooked or not detected. Another emphasis put by criminologists concerns the classification of deviant behaviour. This is not thought to be unequivocal or objective, as the same authorities are involved in both suppressing and registering the behaviour.

In the field of evasion statistics a further problem is generated by the fact that in most countries only a minority of the tax returns is subjected to thorough scrutiny by the authorities. A last point may be made by observing that the tax inspectors' immediate task concerns the maximisation of the output of the tax service in money (tax collected minus costs incurred). This task therefore is *not identical* to maximising the numbers of evaders caught. The tax inspectors use a cost-benefit approach which results in not trying to detect and register evasion when the costs of eventually detecting are estimated to be too high. So at least some of the routine data of the inspectorate may not be ideally suited for research purposes, even when they are optimal from the tax inspectorate's view.

Elffers, Hessing, and Robben (1989) have shown that, at least in Holland, the interjudge reliability of the judgement of the tax authorities is rather low. They carried out an observational study of the auditing of some 900 ordinary tax returns. Over 400 of these were reprocessed by a second official and processed again by a so-called optimal team (three experienced tax officials of different ranks). When the decisions of the various officials were compared the interjudge reliabilities were low: the first and second official agreed in only 59% of cases and the first official and the optimal team agreed in only 52% of cases. The results of the second comparison are particularly interesting since in 39% of cases the optimal team felt the original official had been too lenient. This suggests that regarding official records as 'hard' data may be more than a little optimistic.

2.1.4 Self-reported data

Given the difficulties involved in obtaining access to confidential tax returns or actually observing people completing tax forms, it is not surprising that most research into tax evasion relies on self-report. Economists are generally somewhat suspicious of this kind of data: they think it 'soft', which means it is 'not to be trusted', if not to say 'fishy'. We see this attitude neatly expressed in the opening sentence of a recent article: 'The difficulty of obtaining "hard" empirical data on income-tax evasion has led researchers in this area to *generate their own data* via surveys or experimental simulation' (Baldry 1987, 357 [our emphasis]). We find a different perspective in criminology, however. Criminologists seem to have a rather optimistic view of the reliability of this kind of data, perhaps as a reaction to their discovery that official data are not to be trusted. On the other hand again, social psychologists are doubtful but 'most investigators using such measures have simply acknowledged an awareness of the scepticism surrounding the liability and validity of self-reported data' (Sobell 1976, 2).

In the tax field, we are interested in a particular kind of self-report, namely verbal statements by respondents describing their past behaviour. These have taken a variety of forms. The most simple is the direct question. Wärneryd and Walerud (1982), for example, carried out a telephone survey and asked 'It can often be read in the papers that many people do not report all their incomes or make too large deductions in their income tax returns. Did you ever make a deduction for an expense you had not had or failed to report an income?' Direct questions are often asked in a way that guarantees anonymity. Grasmick and Scott's (1982) respondents recorded their answers on a separate sheet of paper and did not reveal them to the interviewer. This sheet was then sealed in an envelope by the respondent and attached to the questionnaire by the interviewer. To ensure confidentiality, 'locked box' and randomised response methods have been used (McCrohan 1982). In the first, the respondent fills in a self-administered questionnaire and puts it in a locked box. In the second, a respondent is presented with a pair of questions, one on tax behaviour, the other on some innocuous topic and decides which to answer on the toss of a coin. This guarantees anonymity but at the cost of losing a lot of information. Confidentiality can also be obtained with modern technology. For instance, Hessing, Elffers, and Robben (1987) put questions on tax evasion to a tele-interview panel, who are required to answer each week a series of questions on a variety of topics presented to them on a microcomputer.

Despite these attempts to enhance the validity of self-reported tax evasion, past research into deviant behaviour suggests that two main classes of variables will still distort results. These are people's concerns about impression management and their awareness of the behaviour.

It has been argued (Baumeister 1982; Tetlock & Manstead 1985) that a lot of social behaviour can be understood in terms of impression management. That is, people act in certain ways to gain social approval and to construct a personal image congruent with their ideal self. This suggests that inaccurate self-reports may result from concerns about social approval or disapproval and threats to one's self-image. Studies which have compared self-reported behaviour with external criteria have found both over- and underreporting. Overreporting can be the result of a desire to present an image consistent with commonly held social norms (Bell & Buchanan 1966) or norms held by the respondents' reference group (Sudman & Bradburn 1974). Thus Bell and Buchanan (1966) report that 80% of their respondents claimed to have voted in a local election whereas the voter registration records showed that only 50% were eligible to do so. If tax evasion was favoured in a particular social group we might then expect to find respondents boasting about acts of evasion that in fact they have not committed.

Usually researchers into deviant behaviour have been more concerned about underreporting (Phillips 1971). For example, Robins (1963) compared data from official records with interview data in a longitudinal study of deviance. Of 164 people who had been arrested at least once, 30% gave accurate reports, 29% reported fewer arrests than the records showed and 41% denied that they had ever been arrested. This is fairly typical. If respondents know that their answers can or will be checked against other records, their answers tend to be much more accurate (Stephens 1972; Wolfe 1974). Even then, we may expect some distortion because, as Calahan (1968, 621) put it, 'certain questions on past behaviour do not lend themselves to accurate measurement . . . not because people do not want to tell the truth to others but because they cannot tell the truth to themselves'.

There is also the issue of how aware people are of their past behaviour. Self-reports of recent behaviour are unsurprisingly more accurate than those of behaviour that took place in the more distant past (Medanik 1982). Ironically, more severe problems are typically reported more accurately than minor ones (Hood & Sparks 1970). As an example, Guze and Goodwin

(1972) report that individuals with a history of severe drinking problems described this more accurately than those with less pronounced drinking problems. Clearly the more salient a behaviour the easier it is to remember. Since filing a tax return is an annual event at most and evasion is typically for fairly small amounts of money, some inaccuracies in self-reported tax behaviour may well result from respondents not remembering what they have done.

All of this suggests that tax evasion will be underreported and the evidence supports this supposition. We do not have good external criteria, of course. As we discussed above, official records are rather unreliable and so the authorities may well not detect evasion that people are willing to admit in an interview or questionnaire. The official records almost certainly underestimate evasion since tax officials are too lenient (Elffers, Hessing & Robben 1989), and those individuals who evade by not filing their returns are excluded. But a comparison of self-report data with official data reveals that the former show even less evasion. Kinsey (1984) provides some interesting figures. In eighteen separate surveys an average of 20% of respondents admitted evasion. For the same period, United States IRS estimates were that 35% of sampled tax returns showed some evasion. In 1979, an intensive research audit of a sample of returns revealed that 43% had errors that resulted in underpayment of tax. A national survey carried out in the same year on 3,500 respondents found that 27% (locked-box technique) or 32% (randomised-response) admitted evasion.

Obviously it is possible to improve the quality of self-reports. If we ask questions about behaviour that is salient, give convincing assurances of anonymity and also suggest that responses will be checked against records, we should get more accurate results. But on its own self-report data will never give us good estimates of the extent of evasion (something which is true of all methods used to date). This does not matter if self-reports are a good proxy for actual behaviour (if denying tax evasion is randomly distributed throughout the population then results will be conservative but unbiased). Fishbein and Ajzen certainly believe that this is true for behaviour in general: 'we would argue that the use of self-reports goes beyond mere verbal response and provides a meaningful and useful approximation to behaviour *per se*' (1974, 61). They do not, however, give any evidence for this assertion.

The results of studies based on official records and self-reports do correspond in some respects. Both are consistent in finding greater noncompliance among the self-employed, in those with complicated financial situations and in those with income not subject to third-party reports. All these variables reflect differences in the opportunity to evade. But what is really needed is to combine data from official sources with self-reports. The next section discusses this approach.

2.1.5   Combined data

Although the remedy of combining data from the two sources seems obvious, the practical difficulties of doing so have inhibited researchers in the past. For a start, there are privacy and confidentiality restrictions; government agencies are legally bound not to disclose data on individual citizens. Government agencies are also often not happy to see their work scrutinised at an individual level.

The first study which used combined data was that of Schwartz and Orleans (1967). As described in chapter 1, they interviewed people in three different ways about their attitudes to political and civic issues, a month before these people completed their tax returns. The investigators then compared the tax declarations of the three groups. They had no access to official data at an individual level, however, and could use only aggregate information; as they said (1967, 285) 'by giving us distributions for entire groups the IRS complied with the statutory provision that no individual returns be disclosed'. Wallschutzky (1984) came close to combining data: he used officially publicised names of tax offenders but asked his respondents only indirect and hypothetical questions about their tax behaviour (e.g. 'What do you think someone like yourself would do about cash earnings from a part-time job?').

Elffers, Weigel, and Hessing (1987) carried out the first study successfully to combine self-report and official data at an individual level. With the quite exceptional help of the Dutch Ministry of Finance and using a complicated methodology to guarantee confidentiality, they studied two carefully audited groups of individuals selected from a sample of 3,500: one group who had made accurate returns for two years, the other who had evaded tax for two years. The tax returns were not drawn from a random sample but from two separate pools: one a group for whom no additional taxes or corrections had been assessed during the course of the normal auditing procedure for 1981 and 1982, the other a group whose returns had been corrected from whom unpaid back taxes had been collected. The returns were scrutinised by two tax inspectors and only cases where evasion was clearly reproachable and substantial (over 500 guilders) retained in the 'tax evader' category. Those which still required no corrections after the two independent reviews were retained in the nonevader category. There were 342 individuals in each group.

The anonymity of the respondents was carefully protected. The tax authorities sent the individuals' names, addresses and coded tax-return details to a notary and sent the individuals a letter asking them if they would like to take part in the research. Those wishing to participate replied to the notary, who then released the names and addresses (but not the tax-return details) to the researchers. During the interview respondents noted their answers down on a separate form, which was sent to the notary. He then coupled the coded tax-return details with the respondents' data, removed names and addresses and sent the complete data to the researchers. Finally, the tax authorities revealed the decoding key for the tax returns. All of this ensured that at no time did the authorities, the notary, or the researcher know all three chunks of information about an individual, i.e. identification, tax-evasion status, and interview data.

This rather cumbersome procedure led to a rather low response rate (23% overall) but there are good reasons for believing the participants to be reasonably representative of the original categories. First, those individuals who were finally revealed to be evaders were nearly as likely to participate as the nonevaders (21% compared to 25%). Second, the average amount of money evaded did not differ significantly between those evaders who participated and those who did not.

Despite the safeguarding of respondents' anonymity (which should have minimised the effect of impression management) the results showed that documented and self-reported tax evasion did not correspond at all. The correlation between self-reported evasion and documented evasion was 0.06, and -0.03 for the relation between self-report and the amount of taxes paid back. There were inconsistencies between the self-report and official data in 45% of cases. As might be expected, this was less in the nonevader group, where 25% reported some misrepresentation of income or deductions, than in the evader group, where 69% denied evading taxes in either year. Evasion was usually denied even by the most flagrant evaders: among those whose audits resulted in corrections of more than a thousand guilders (approximately £330) in both 1981 and 1982, more than 70% denied misrepresenting income or deductions in either year.

There are good reasons for expecting the self-report data in this study to be reasonably accurate. The behaviour was probably salient for the respondents, at least for the evader group, who had had to pay back taxes two years in a row (this is fairly unusual; see Drost & Jongman 1982). Anonymity had been guaranteed and the respondent's actual tax liabilities had been exposed and resolved without protest. Furthermore the respondents were willing volunteers.

There are also good reasons for expecting the official data to be reasonably accurate. Although Elffers, Hessing, and Robben (1989) have shown that the validity and reliability of routine tax-return processing in the Netherlands is quite low and errs on the lenient side, the criteria adopted in this study were far more stringent. It is true that appealing against the decisions of the tax authorities can be expensive and time-consuming and so some of the evader group may have acquiesced rather than agreed with the judgement of the authorities. But this seems likely to apply to only a minority of this group.

So what are we to make of these findings? They certainly suggest that obtaining accurate self-reports about personally sensitive information is difficult. In this case, it could be that those in the evader group who deny evasion are concerned about prosecution. 'Intentionality' is a crucial factor in the legal definition of evasion. This was very evident in the recent prosecution in Britain of the entertainer Ken Dodd, where the defendant did not deny that he owed the authorities unpaid back taxes, but was emphatic that he had not intended to defraud the Inland Revenue. So, if they are at all suspicious of the guaranteed anonymity, respondents may be wary of admitting evasion.

It is also possible that some of the sample had forgotten their earlier evasion. Two small unpublished studies mentioned by Hessing, Robben, and Elffers (1989) provide some evidence for this view. In 1986 they asked a sample of Dutch taxpayers (using the telepanel technique) about their evasion behaviour in 1985. In 1988 they approached this sample again, asking about their tax behaviour in the previous three years. It was possible to get 207 respondents who had taken part in the 1986 panel to take part again in 1988. In 1986, 11% (22) of the 207 respondents admitted tax evasion in 1985. In 1988, 8% (17) admitted to evading taxes at least once in the previous three years (1987, 1986, and 1985). Of the 22 respondents who admitted tax evasion in 1986 (about tax year 1985), 18 did not remember any more in 1988, or denied that they evaded taxes in 1985.

The results also cast considerable doubt on the logic underlying Fishbein and Ajzen's (1975) model. Very briefly, the substantive results of this study (see Hessing, Elffers & Weigel 1988) show that personality variables (alienation, competitiveness, tolerance of illegal behaviour, combining into a self-serving orientation index) predict documented evasion whereas attitudes towards the act of evasion and subjective norms correlate with self-reported evasion. Initially, Fishbein and Ajzen (1975) were more concerned with the prediction of behavioural intentions but in its later versions (Ajzen & Fishbein 1980) their theory is clearly in the business of predicting behaviour. In this context at least, self-reports do not, as they claim, 'provide a useful approximation to behaviour'.

So it is not possible to take at face value respondents' answers to the question of whether or not they have evaded taxes when filing a tax return. This issue has been explored further by Kinsey (1988). She carried out a secondary analysis of an IRS-sponsored survey to see if the pattern of results reported by Hessing, Elffers, and Weigel could be replicated. Although there was not an exact match between the measures of attitudes, subjective norms, and personality variables used in the IRS survey and by Hessing, Elffers, and Weigel, Kinsey was able to construct scales which corresponded quite well. As a proxy for documented evasion, she used self-reported audit outcome. So respondents who reported having paid more taxes as the result of a tax examination were treated as 'officially defined' tax evaders. Those who admitted noncompliance in the previous five years were treated as self-reported evaders. The results obtained were comparable to those of Hessing, Elffers, and Weigel: the attitude and subjective norm measures correlated with self-reported evasion and not with self-reported audit outcome, and conversely one of the personality attributes (tolerance of illegal behaviour) correlated with self-reported audit outcome and not self-reported evasion. The other personality variable used (alienation) had the same pattern of correlations as the attitude measures.

Kinsey concludes that the findings of Hessing, Elffers and Weigel are therefore robust but that documented tax evasion should not be the benchmark by which other forms of measurement should be assessed. On the contrary, these two studies raise questions about how evasion is perceived by taxpayers and the authorities and imply that 'it is conceptually more consistent with the socially-constructed nature of noncompliance to view it as consisting of judgements and claims about behaviour than as a behaviour in and of itself' (Kinsey 1988, 19). Our own view is that, although noncompliance is a social construction, it is not just a social construction; taxpayers are, after all, taking decisions and acting upon them. To go further we need to know more about what variables predict different 'kinds' of evasion.

Although interesting from the theoretical and methodological points of view, combining data from self-reports and official records is not an easy option. On the contrary, the confidentiality restrictions make the procedure cumbersome, which in turn leads to considerable (and probably nonrandom) subject attrition. Even more crucial is the fact that the active cooperation of the tax authorities is essential. We already know that the tax authorities in several countries would be unwilling or unable to cooperate in such studies. In Holland, where the tax inspectorate is in principle not unwilling, they cannot repeatedly be asked for assistance, at least not for routine research. So there is a need for alternative ways of gathering data on tax evasion. Experimental approaches are one possibility.

2.2   The experimental approach

Both economists and psychologists share a recently developed interest in the experimental approach to tax evasion, and indeed the first such study was the result of a collaboration between researchers from the two disciplines (Friedland, Maital & Rutenberg 1978). Experimental methods have been seen by some economists as a reasonably unproblematic way of 'generating data' (Baldry 1987), but despite the burgeoning interest in experimental economics (see Roth 1986, 1987; Smith 1987), acceptance of laboratory findings by mainstream economics is far from universal. By way of contrast, social psychology is largely based on experiments: Tajfel and Fraser (1978) estimate that at least two-thirds of all social psychological studies are experimental. None the less, experiments have been subjected to considerable criticism within social psychology in recent years (e.g. Silverman 1977) and there has been a growing use of alternative methods.

Our advocacy of an experimental approach to the study of tax evasion therefore may seem to some to be slightly retrograde. But we are making a fairly modest claim: that suitably designed experiments can complement research using surveys and official records and are particularly useful in untangling causal mechanisms. 'Suitably designed' is of course a rather empty phrase. To fill it with some meaning we will first look closely at past studies and some of the methodological problems involved. Then we shall take a wider look at the general advantages and disadvantages of the approach.

Friedland, Maital, and Rutenberg (1978) pioneered the use of experiments in this area. They carried out a fairly small-scale study in which student subjects were given tax tables and then received a monthly income which they had to declare so as to maximise net income. The experiment had a 2×2 design with tax rates (25%, 50%) and frequency of auditing/severity of fine as independent variables. They found that large fines (with a small probability of detection) were a more effective deterrent than small fines (with a high probability of detection). In a very similar follow-up study, Friedland (1982) found that vague information about the probability of audits enhances their deterrent value. Spicer and Thomas' (1982) study of audit probabilities was very similar in design to that of Friedland, Maital, and Rutenberg. They found that changing audit probabilities seemed to change individuals' propensity to cheat but not the amount of taxes they evaded.

Two other studies by Spicer also followed the Friedland, Maital, and Rutenberg set-up very closely. Spicer and Becker (1980) looked at the effect of two variables: equity and a measure of tax resistance. All subjects used tax tables based on a rate of 40%, but one third were told that this was the average rate, another third that the average rate was 65% and the final third that the average rate was 15%. This manipulation was devised to induce feelings of advantageous and disadvantageous equity. These feelings had a strong effect; the group that believed the average rate to be 15% evaded the highest percentage of tax whilst the group which believed the average rate to be 65% evaded the lowest percentage. The individual differences in tax resistance did not produce any clear result.

Spicer and Hero (1985) examined the relationship between evasion and perceived evasion by others and audit occurrence. Subjects were given fictitious information about the behaviour of participants in a previous study, namely that they had paid 10%, 50% or 90% of taxes due. This information had no effect on evasion, whereas the number of prior audits had a negative effect.

These five studies use almost identical procedures and consequently have similar flaws. All use small samples of students as subjects. There are good reasons for being wary of such samples in general, and in the tax case this is particularly true since experience of the tax system may well be important. All use a very simple situation in which all participants do is to declare tax. This makes the purpose of the experiments transparent: the participants' only task was to declare an income and virtually the only information they received concerned tax rates, audit frequencies and fine rates. In all cases they are given instructions which bias the findings by defining the situation in a particular way. This can be seen if we consider the instructions used by Friedland, Maital, and Rutenberg: 'This research takes the form of an economic game. In general, each one of you will receive salary slips. You will be asked to report your income, and pay income tax on the income you reported. From time to time, audits will be conducted according to a random sample and fines imposed on tax evaded. At the end of each round of 10 months each person's net income will be added up (gross income less income tax less fines). The objective of the game is to accumulate the maximum amount of net income.'

Two points can be made about these instructions. First, the only way of making this into an interesting and involving 'game' is to gamble, to declare less income than you have earned and enjoy the excitement of seeing if you can get away with it. Having got involved, the only relevant factors are the fine rate and audit frequency; moral considerations are irrelevant. Second, the stated objective is to maximise net income. This is a rather obvious bias towards the models of rational optimising which these experiments claim to be testing.

Webley and Halstead (1986) carried out three studies which were very similar in form to the five studies described above except for the important difference that the experiments were implemented on a microcomputer. This made the procedure more efficient since calculations of subjects' tax liability and random audits were all carried out by the computer. It also meant that the task could be made more interesting for the participants: features like a tax man who travelled across the screen and occasionally entered the subjects' 'house' and red text when a subject was discovered cheating were included. However, the essential features of the Friedland, Maital, and Rutenberg style studies were preserved.

Webley and Halstead found that when the situation was defined as a 'problem' rather than as a 'game' subjects optimised more efficiently. More importantly, their postexperimental interviews suggested that most people saw the situation as a game, and a minority saw it as a tax-declaring situation or as an optimising situation. Those who saw the situation as a tax-declaring one were almost entirely honest, and accounted for their decisions by stating that it was 'wrong' to cheat, and that there would be 'too much aggro if you were caught'. Those who perceived the situation as a game tended to use partial declarations of income whereas those subjects optimising tended to use an all-or-nothing approach to declaring. This suggests that we should be very cautious about generalising from all of the experiments described so far since their external validity is doubtful.

Recent experiments by economists have used different kinds of procedures and raise some interesting questions (Güth & Mackscheidt 1985; Baldry 1986, 1987; Becker, Büchner & Sleeking 1987). Güth and Mackscheidt were concerned with the impact of public transfer expenditures on tax evasion (these are expenditures which redistribute money from some taxpayers to others, e.g. child allowances). They used a progressive tax rate, and transfers depended on the actual total revenue of taxes. Becker, Büchner, and Sleeking also explored the effect of transfers and looked at the effect of income, expected audit probability and perceived tax burden. Their design was based on that of Güth and Mackscheidt, with a number of modifications intended to 'better simulate reality'. Their transfer payments depended on the expected sum of all tax payments (since in real economies transfers are based on expected public revenue), audit probability was not known to the participants, and participants had to 'work' for their income. This work was the solving of a series of mathematical problems. Furthermore, if the sum of tax and fine was greater than the sum of pretax income and transfer payment, participants had to pay out of their own pocket.

Becker, Büchner and Sleeking found that the propensity to evade taxes rises with increasing income, falls with rising transfer payments and is negatively correlated with expected audit probability. Only the latter significantly influenced the amount of taxes evaded. They point out that the results must be treated cautiously as participants may act differently in the experiment than in reality. Two features relevant to this are singled out: the artificiality of the experimental situation and the fact that the effect of stigmatisation are excluded.

This series of experiments is certainly more sophisticated than the Friedland, Maital, and Rutenberg clones. A serious attempt was made to incorporate aspects of economic reality, both to provide a better test of the economic model (as with the change in the operationalisation of transfers) and to ensure that participants' behaviour in the experiment corresponded with that outside of it (the introduction of 'work'). The purpose of the experiment was still very obvious, however, and the use of economics students as subjects (who presumably have some grasp of conventional theory) exacerbates this problem.

Baldry's (1986, 1987) experiments focus on similar issues but use an intriguingly different procedure. The experiments took place over an extended period (six 'rounds' over two weeks). At the end of a class participants were given an envelope containing information about their income for that round, details of how to calculate their tax liability, and a tax return. They had to complete the tax return and hand it in at the beginning of the next class. This means that participants completed their tax forms when and where they wished and they could consult others or use calculators if they were so inclined. The tax forms that were used imitated the style of Australian tax returns.

Baldry's aim was fairly straightforward: to set up the standard economic model in an unambiguous form and test its predictions. He concluded that the model is inadequate because moral considerations seem to reduce evasion and the tax schedule itself (particularly high marginal tax rates) has an effect on evasion. In addition, the 1986 experiments showed that identical decision problems dressed up in different ways (as a tax problem or a simple gamble) are reacted to differently. We would have no quarrel with these conclusions except that there are some methodological aspects which deserve discussion. Perhaps the most interesting issue is that of payment.

In both Baldry's and Becker, Büchner, and Sleeking's studies subjects were paid real money and paid taxes on this money. In Baldry's 1987 experiments, honest subjects could expect to earn $2.40 or $3.00 (depending on which group they were in), though participants could earn a lot more (the highest paid received $6.78). Becker, Büchner, and Sleeking's subjects earned between 2 and 16 Deutschmarks (approximately $1.00 to $8.00). The tax schedules used were scaled-down versions of the real thing; in one of Baldry's an income of up to 15 cents per round was exempt from tax, for from 15 to 45 cents the tax rate was 30%, and above 45 cents it was 65%. These rewards may be contrasted with the method of payment used by Webley and Halstead (1986), where money prizes were given to the people with the largest net income, and with the method generally used in our studies, where people are paid for participating rather than by results.

Setting up the situation so that evasion can lead to a real monetary loss or gain is seen as crucial by economists. For example, Baldry (personal communication), commenting on the Webley and Halstead studies, points out that, if subjects are told that the most successful volunteers will get a prize, they will compete against each other rather than against the tax authorities and this will destroy the realism of the experiment. He believes that subjects should have enough information to calculate the probability distribution of the monetary outcomes for each decision they may make.

Though this analysis of the Webley and Halstead method of payment may well be correct, in our view monetary payment is secondary to involvement.

If participants are involved or psychologically engaged in the situation their decisions will be meaningful. They do not need to be taking decisions about real money. It may even be counterproductive to have people taking decisions in terms of cents, pennies or pfennigs, since this emphasises the relative triviality of the decisions that are being made. The evidence from the social dilemmas literature (Dawes 1980) supports this view, and such comparative experiments as have been carried out show few differences in results when real rather than imaginary payoffs are used.

2.2.1   *The experimental approach: A wider perspective*

The general idea of an experimental approach to studying tax-paying behaviour is extremely simple. Ideally we would manipulate the environment in which people perform the behaviour under study, observe that behaviour and then draw appropriate conclusions. A good example in a different economic context is Raj's (1982) study of the effect on sales of increased advertising of one brand in a market dominated by two brands. He was lucky enough to have access to a split-cable TV system, where comparable households are connected to one of two cables. But because it is not feasible to manipulate the environment where people earn their money and declare their income, we have to have recourse to an artificial environment, and study behaviour in a setting that can be controlled by the experimenter. This is commonplace and there are plenty of examples of research using business games (e.g. DeJong, Forsythe & Uecker 1988), laboratory experiments on freerider behaviour (e.g. Liebrand 1984), and so on.

The great advantage of this method is well known. It is that we can isolate the variables we are interested in and study the effects of our manipulations knowing that these are not the result of extraneous factors. No other method is as good at untangling the causal structure of a phenomenon. There are also a number of lesser practical advantages. Artificial environments can be more easily manipulated by the experimenter than real-life situations; complex tasks can be condensed into manageable abstractions; people can be put into situations where ordinarily they cannot be observed; and the method will be cheaper than a field study in most cases.

Set against these advantages are some very real disadvantages. The artificial nature of experiments is probably the commonest criticism in both psychology and economics and this usually leads to comments about their lack of external validity. Brookshire, Coursey, and Schulze (1987) reckon that when experimental economists present their work at conferences the typical response is to question whether the results apply to 'real-world' settings. People are right to worry about external validity but not because of artificiality. As Doise (1986, 145) put it, 'Like the artist, the experimenter does not attempt to produce a naturalistic representation of reality or a perfect correspondence between the details of the experimental situation and those of reality outside. On the contrary, as in pictures by Munch, Nolde or Permeke, an apparent disfiguring of reality in an experiment may express an aspect of the socially real more strongly.' In other words, artificiality *per se* does not matter as long as the important variables have been operationalised so that they engage the same psychological processes as their real-world counterparts.

This seems straightforward but in practice it is hard to ensure that our operationalisations are doing just that. How can we know that the laboratory model of the economic process under study is realistic? Aronson and Carlsmith (1968) pointed out that an experiment can be realistic in two ways. If it has an impact on the participants, if they are involved in it and take it seriously, if it evokes the same processes that it is trying to model, then the researcher has achieved 'experimental realism'. If the experimental situation resembles the real world closely we have 'mundane realism'. It is quite possible for an experiment to have mundane realism but poor experimental realism. In some experiments into gambling, for instance, a casino situation was reproduced in an apparently convincing manner, but the behavioural and autonomic responses of habitual gamblers were very different to those that they showed in the real-life situation (Anderson & Brown 1984). Conversely, an experiment may have little mundane realism yet excellent experimental realism. Milgram's (1974) studies of obedience are a good example. Mundane realism may often help to ensure experimental realism but it does not guarantee it.

None of the tax-evasion experiments that we described above had much mundane realism, although mundane features were used in some of them (e.g. Baldry's imitation of Australian tax forms). Their experimental realism is debatable; that subjects take the situation seriously (mentioned in many of the reports) is a necessary but not sufficient condition. It is quite possible for an experiment unintentionally to shed light on a different phenomenon. Thus a tax-evasion experiment might be quite a good study of factors that affect optimising or cheating, but not capture the psychological processes that are involved in evasion.

One reason for this shortfall, and a major problem for all experimentation in social science, is that the experiment itself is a social situation. People are not passive and may alter their behaviour because they are taking part in an experiment. This might involve doing what they think is desired by the experimenter (Orne 1962), behaving in ways that make them look good or, in some cases, being negative and uncooperative (Masling 1966). As well as these differences in subject roles, experiments may differ in what Orne called 'demand characteristics'. This term covers the many aspects of the experimental situation that subjects can use to guess the aim of the experiments. If subjects can ascertain what the experimenter wants to show and are motivated and able to help, we cannot be sure that an experimental effect is genuine. The rationality framework which underpins much work in experimental economics seems especially likely to provide cues to individuals that they should behave in a particular way. So, unless these experiments are carefully designed, the results may reflect a person's understanding of economics rather than the behaviour that would be displayed in the real situation.

Demand characteristics have clearly been a problem with previous experiments into tax evasion. In all cases it is obvious what the experiment is about. This does not mean that participants were aware of the hypotheses or understood the nature of the manipulations, but that the focus on evasion was evident. (This is not quite true. Baldry (1987) reports that one subject in his study thought that the experiment was designed to see if students could complete tax returns properly.) It is not enough to carry out postexperimental interviews to see how the experiment was perceived: it is difficult to check whether demand characteristics are affecting results because of the nature of the implicit contract between experimenter and participant. If there is an implicit understanding that the participants will be 'good' subjects, they may well not acknowledge in a postexperimental questionnaire or interview that they had identified the purpose of the study and behaved accordingly. We believe that it is crucial for the purpose of the experiments to be opaque. This is not easy to achieve since the experimental setting must involve taxation, and the caricatured nature of manipulations can inadvertently reveal the rationale which lies behind them. Operationalisations cannot be too subtle or else they will pass unnoticed. They must not be too obvious for then they reveal the point of the study and cooperative subjects will give us the results we want. Our basic solution to this problem is to set up small-business simulations in which the declaration of income for tax purposes is just one of a series of decisions that participants have to make.

This creates a further difficulty for, even if the respondents do react in the experiment as they would do in normal life, if it models a situation that is unusual for them, or is outside their experience, it is hard to know what to make of their behaviour. Only a minority of people have experience of running small businesses and most students and many women (in Britain) have no experience of filling in tax forms. This difficulty is one that is often encountered in other areas with certain kinds of questionnaires: in its general form the question is, what sense can we make of people's answers to hypothetical questions? Indeed, Van der Pligt (1986) has argued that people's answers to the kinds of hypothetical questions used by Kahnemann and Tversky (1984) to test prospect theory do not correspond to their responses to similar everyday versions. What we believe is crucial here is a distinction between the rather passive responses to hypothetical questions on a questionnaire and the active response to the hypothetical decisions required in our small-business simulations.

There are two remaining general issues that deserve discussion. These are the problem of sampling and the actual dependent measures to be used. Sampling is always a problem, but it is more of a problem in experimental research. In a self-report study you normally investigate people who are at least involved in the behaviour being studied. In experimental research this is not true: researchers often just use the subjects at hand. It is well known that most psychological knowledge rests on studies of college students. Jung (1982) reports that 90% of human subjects used by American psychology departments were students and 73% were taking introductory psychology courses. So it is not surprising that tax-evasion experiments are generally carried out on economics or psychology students. But, although this may not matter in certain areas of psychology, students are a rather unsatisfactory sample for studies of tax behaviour. This does not mean experiments with students are useless but that they require careful interpretation. Ideally, one needs to check if different subject pools (e.g. students, the general public, businessmen) exhibit different behaviour in the same experiment (see DeJong, Forsythe & Uecker 1988).

The final issue is what one should actually observe. Like much else in social psychology experiments, the dependent measures used are often caricatures of the real behaviour to which they correspond. This is not a criticism: good caricatures capture and exaggerate the essential features of an individual. It is not obvious what would constitute a good dependent measure in a tax-evasion experiment, especially if the behaviour is conceived, following Smith and Kinsey's (1987) strictures, as a process rather than as an event. In all the experiments described above (and in many of our own studies) subjects have only to declare their given income. They can declare what percentage of it they like but they cannot simply fail to file a return (one strategy for evading tax). There are no opportunities to claim false deductions or consider what to do about income from other sources like a second job. We have no panaceas but we believe now that a series of repetitious and simplified income declarations is probably a rather poor dependent measure, since people do not have the opportunity to evade in ways that they may consider more acceptable.

To put some flesh on the bare bones of our argument, we now describe the first of our studies in which the evasion decision was embedded within a business simulation. As with the Webley and Halstead (1986) experiments, this, and all the others to be described, are implemented on a microcomputer. Whether this materially affects the results of the experiment will be considered in the next section.

2.3   A first example, UK04: Tax evasion in a small-business simulation

This example was a study carried out in 1985 on a sample of students in Exeter (UK). The study simply aimed to replicate some of the previous findings – such as the effect of audit probabilities and penalties – by Friedland, Maital, and Rutenberg (1978). The main deviations from previous studies were that the tax aspect was made less obvious and the choice of evading a less obligatory one. It uses a repetitious dependent measure but hopefully suffers less from demand characteristics as its purpose is less obvious.

Forty-six undergraduates taking psychology as an ancillary subject were recruited as participants. They were tested in four batches. They were asked to sit down at a computer and to type in their subject number (which they had been assigned at random). This number determined which of the experimental conditions they were in. One condition had a fine rate of twice the amount of tax evaded, the other a fine rate of six times. All subjects participated over two 'years'. Each year had a different stated audit probability, either 1 in 6 or 3 in 6. Half of the subjects in each condition were given the 1 in 6 followed by the 3 in 6 probability, the other half were given the reverse order. Audit occurrence was determined randomly based on the appropriate probability, so that some participants were never audited whereas others were audited four times in one year. Audit occurrence was matched in the two experimental conditions. The subject received the following instructions on the screen:

> This is an economic simulation. You are to imagine that after graduation from Exeter University you set yourself up as a landscape gardener.
>
> You will have to make a series of decisions over a two year period. For example, you will have to decide how much per hour to charge for your services, whether to advertise or not and whether you want any market research carried out. You will also have to report your income and pay tax on the amount reported.
>
> Each year is divided into 6 two month periods. Each period you will be asked to do four things. These are:
> 1. decide whether or not you want to buy information, and if so, what kind.
> 2. decide whether or not you want to advertise for that period and, if so how much you will spend.
> 3. set your charge per hour for that two month period.
> 4. make a tax return. (The bank has granted overdraft facilities for the first period.)

INFORMATION

Information is of six kinds and costs £50 per bit. You may buy only 1 bit of information per period. You may buy the following information:
1. what your competitors are charging.
2. market research on consumers.
3. a geological survey of the area.
4. forecasts of likely tax changes.
5. forecasts of trends in the market.
6. agency research on the effectiveness of advertising.

ADVERTISING

Advertising costs £80 per unit. You may purchase up to 5 units per period.

CHARGES

You may charge any amount per hour that you wish, but at high prices you will get too little custom, and at low prices too much (you may only work a 40-hour week).

TAXATION

At the end of each period your total receipts will be calculated. You will be asked to report your taxable income (receipts minus advertising and information costs). The tax rate is 30%. From time to time, audits will be conducted according to a random sample, and fines imposed on tax evaded.

If you are drawn in the random sample then you will be audited. If you underreported income then, for this period only, you will be fined x [with x being 2 or 6 depending on experimental condition] times the amount of tax evaded. At the end of the game, everybody's net income will be calculated. Money prizes will be distributed according to people's net income. Would you like to read through the instructions again? If so, type Y, if not type N and the game will begin.

In each period participants would be asked to make the four decisions (about buying information, advertising, setting charges and declaring income) described above. For example, in the first period a person might pay for information about 'what your competitors are charging' and would then see the following:

THE COMPETITION

There are four firms operating in your area, as follows:
1. Foxwells. This is a long-established local firm who provide what they call a total service. Landscape gardening is just one of their activities (they also run the largest local garden centre). They charge £7 an hour for their total service.
2. Elliot Design Ltd. This is a national firm, recently featured in the *Sunday Times*. They charge £15 an hour for a consultation.

3. Tony Plato. He is a graduate with no specific horticultural training. He charges £3 an hour.
4. John Ample. He is a trained gardener who has recently set up on his own. He charges £4.50 an hour.

They might decide to buy three units of advertising (£80 a unit) and charge £3.50 an hour. There would then be a graphic display of the number of hours of orders (spades printed across the screen). At this price the subject would obtain 60 hours of orders (an overfull order book) and have takings of £1,120 (40 hours × £3.50 × 8 weeks). The following would then be displayed on the screen:

It is year 1, period 1. The average audit frequency is 1 in 6.
Your balance sheet this period is as follows:
    Total receipts   £1120
    Total costs   £290
    Taxable income   £820

How much income do you declare?

After the income declaration, there was a graphic display of a tax man walking across the screen in front of a house. If he entered the house, this indicated an audit; if he walked past there was no audit. Gross income, net income and total fines paid were then displayed and the next period began.

Completing the session took between twenty minutes and an hour, the average being approximately thirty-five minutes.

Two quantitative measures of the participant's behaviour were taken: the frequency of underdeclaring and the percentage of income declared (using an arc-sine transformation). These data were analysed using two mixed analyses of variance with fine severity (two levels) as a between-groups factor, and audit probability (two levels) as a within-groups factor. An arc-sine transformation was used to transform the percentage figures (Winer 1971). The tables however, show untransformed figures, for ease of understanding. This remark applies throughout the book. As Table 2.1 indicates, the severity of fine had no significant effect on either the percentage of income declared or the number of periods that tax was evaded ($F = 1.5$, NS; $F = 0.05$, NS). Audit probability did significantly affect percentage of income declared ($F = 5.8$, $p < 0.05$) and number of periods that tax was evaded ($F = 20.1$, $p < 0.01$). Interactions in both cases were nonsignificant.

Higher audit probabilities therefore lead to less tax evasion (as previous studies have shown) but there was no evidence that this effect is specific to the number of occasions people evaded, as Spicer and Thomas (1982) found. Severity of fine had no effect (a result also found by Webley and Halstead 1986) but this could be due to the comparatively small difference in the fine rates used. Friedland, Maital, and Rutenberg (1978), by way of comparison,

Table 2.1. *Mean percentage of income not declared as a function of severity of fine and audit probability (N=46)*

Audit probability		1 in 6	3 in 6	Overall
Severity of fine	2 ×	27	18	22
	6 ×	16	10	13
Overall		21	14	18

Table 2.2. *Mean number of times (out of 12) that income was underdeclared as a function of severity of fine and audit probability (N=46)*

Audit probability		1 in 6	3 in 6	Overall
Severity of fine	2 ×	3.7	2.9	3.3
	6 ×	3.9	2.9	3.4
Overall		3.8	2.9	3.3

Table 2.3. *Income underdeclared in the penultimate period regressed on income underdeclared in the first period and the number of prior audits (t-values in brackets, N=46)*

	Standardised regression coefficient
Income underdeclared in first period	0.31* (2.2)
Number of prior audits	−0.20 (1.4)
$R^2 = 0.16$	

*significant at a 5% level

used fine rates of 15 × and 3 ×. Another possibility is that in previous studies the fine rate was more salient as it changed during the course of the experiment.

Friedland, Maital, and Rutenberg (1978) reported that large fines with a low audit probability lead to less tax evasion than mathematically equivalent small fines coupled with a higher audit probability. There is no evidence in this study for this effect; in fact tax is evaded less often with a 2 × fine rate with a 3 in 6 audit probability than with a 6 × fine rate with a 1 in 6 audit probability (see Table 2.2).

The amount of income underdeclared in the penultimate (eleventh) period was regressed on the amount of income underdeclared in the first period and the number of audits in the first ten periods. The penultimate period was chosen as it was believed that behaviour in the last period might be atypical. The amount of income underdeclared in the penultimate period was significantly positively related to the amount of income underdeclared in the first period, whereas the number of audits was related negatively but nonsignificantly (see Table 2.3). The pattern of these results is comparable to that found by Spicer and Hero (1985), although the relationships are weaker. It must be borne in mind that for all participants the audit probability was different on the penultimate to that on the first period.

The experiment supports the propositions that audit probability and individual differences are predictors of tax evasion in a business simulation and it provides some support for Spicer and Hero's claim that being audited lowers tax evasion even when audits are made at random.

Leaving aside any substantive findings, the crucial difference between this and previous experimental studies is that here subjects are making a number of financial decisions and it is not so obvious to them what the study is about. The fact that the simulation is set up on a computer may give some concern. Baldry (personal communication) has said that he feels it advisable not to run a tax experiment on a computer for three reasons: the relevant real-life situation generally does not involve the use of computers, the computer screen and keyboard 'come between the situation and the subject' and the computer is more likely to be seen as a gaming machine than as an aid to efficiency. The first point is of little significance unless the use of computers excludes some important factor. One possible candidate is the fact that individuals completing real tax forms have to sign a declaration that their return is accurate. The second point we would argue is misplaced. Rather than 'coming between' the situation and the subject, the keyboard and screen are the way in which the subject is involved in the situation. The responses required are simple (pressing numbers or the space bar) and participants do not need to be familiar with computers to take part effectively. In later experiments we added information on the use of the computer at the outset to obviate any problems caused by lack of familiarity, and in our final experiments we used practice sessions as well. The third point is a serious concern, however, given the number of Webley and Halstead's (1986) subjects who reported seeing the situation as a game. We feel that it is not the computer *per se* that conveys the message that the situation is a game but the content of the program. For that reason, the graphic display of the taxman was removed from all later versions of the 'landscape gardener' simulation and business aspects were stressed in the instructions for the shop simulations. Finally, it should be noted that the question 'How much income do you declare' was meant to be a neutral question, simply referring to the total amount to be declared. Since the computer – in the perception of the respondent – would not be able to know how much money the respondent had made, the computer simply asked 'How much income do you declare' as in 'How much money did you make last year.' In following simulations (see 3.3) this question was replaced by 'How much of your TAXABLE INCOME do you want to declare?' The change in the wording of that question was meant to make it (more) clear to the subjects that there was a possibility to evade, since it could be understood as follows: (1) There is a taxable income, and (2) it is possible to declare only part of that taxable income.

2.4   Conclusions

We believe that experimental methods have a role to play in research on tax evasion. To do so they must be well designed of course, but in addition they must be embedded in a theory which explains tax evasion in the abstract and tax evasion as measured by self-report, official records, and experiments. In itself multiple measurement does not get us very far. Many years ago Webb, Campbell, Schwartz, and Sechrest (1966) emphasised the value of using multiple indicators and diverse collection procedures and stressed the notion of triangulation. This derives from cartography and navigation: the basic idea is that by taking sightings from different places we can pinpoint the location of the unexplored volcano, mysterious temple, or what have you. The problem is that this assumes that we are certain about the location of our sighting points and that the temple isn't so mysterious that it wanders around from day to day. As Blalock (1982) put it, 'triangulation is impossible without an explicit and rather precise theory concerning the properties of triangulation – multiple measures without a theory will only lead to chaotic results'.

In a different although relevant context (people's accounts of their behaviour), Potter and Wetherall (1987) suggest that triangulation often leads to 'homing out' rather than 'homing in'. Instead of finding a core account which represents an individual's 'real' beliefs, a wide variety of nonoverlapping accounts are obtained. This leads them to question the notion of 'real' beliefs and there is a similar debate about whether one can talk about 'real' tax evasion (see Kinsey, 1988). We suspect that this kind of relativism is a dead end. Instead we favour replacing the metaphor of triangulation with that of simultaneous equations. The values of all variables are initially unknown but, with enough equations, we can determine their values. Thus we have officially recorded evasion (which can be predicted by a theory of tax evasion plus a theory of how tax officials operate), self-reported evasion (predicted by the self-same theory of evasion and a theory about presentational concerns), and experimental evasion (theory of evasion plus a knowledge of the social psychology of experiments).

Things are not quite that simple, of course. The theory needs to make sense of behaviour within and outside of experiments and it needs to explicate people's accounts of their in- and out-experiment behaviour. But we do have the beginnings of such an approach. We have a theory of tax evasion (that of Weigel, Hessing & Elffers 1987) and a theory of how self-presentational concerns affect self-reported behaviour (Hessing, Elffers & Weigel 1988). Our strategy with experiments has been to strive to minimise demand effects and the like and to improve experimental realism so that the results cohere with our other studies.

We have had one further thing in mind. Eiser (1986, 342) points out that 'an experiment is like a radio: if we twiddle the knobs at random, there's no telling what we will find, nor any guarantee that it will be in a language we understand, even though the radio itself may be in perfect working order. On the other hand, if the radio is accurately tuned, we can expect to hear something, and also, which is especially important, we can expect others whose radios are similarly tuned to hear the same thing.' In other words (and more prosaically) replication is crucial. Despite the problems involved in cross-national studies in the taxation field (even deciding which tax rate to use is difficult), we have generally tried to carry out identical studies in Holland and Britain.

The three empirical chapters in this monograph are rather different. The first describes our earlier studies which are based on social psychological theory (social comparison and equity) and in which participants can only evade tax by declaring less income. A secondary focus is the role of individual differences in attitudes and personality. The second empirical chapter concentrates on the processes involved in deciding to evade and most of the studies described use a more complex set-up where participants can evade tax both by underdeclaring income and claiming unwarranted allowances. Here the theoretical basis is Kahneman and Tversky's (1984) prospect theory. A recurrent theme in both of these chapters is the validity of the experimental approach, which is confronted directly in the third empirical chapter.

3 Social comparison, equity, attitudes, and tax evasion

3.1 Introduction

This chapter reports four studies carried out between 1985 and 1987 which explore the question of whether social comparison processes (including equity) are implicated in tax evasion as both theory (Adams 1965; Rijsman 1983) and respondents' self-report would suggest. In addition, two of the studies look at the correlates of evasion in an experimental setting. Study UK05 investigated the effect of perceived inequity and earnings comparisons on evasion. Study UK06 examined the effect of perceived inequity and whether the nature of comparison (individual or social) was important. Study UK07 took this further by using a general public sample and obtaining measures of some of the attitudinal variables that predict documented and self-reported tax evasion. Study NL01 is a replication of UK07 carried out in Holland. The rationale for the UK numbering system is that studies preceding the ones reported in this book are described in Webley and Halstead (1986).

To set the scene we will review the relevant material under three headings: equity, social comparison, and individual differences.

3.1.1 *Equity and tax evasion*

The taxpayer–government relationship can be seen as involving an exchange: the taxpayer pays his or her taxes and national insurance contributions and the government supplies various benefits, such as health care and education. There is considerable evidence in other domains (see Adams & Freedman 1976) that, if an exchange is seen as unfair, individuals will take steps to redress the balance. For example, people work less if they perceive themselves as underpaid and, less obviously, those perceiving themselves as overpaid work harder than those paid the 'normal' amount (Lawler 1968). If we extend this approach to the tax context, we can see that tax evasion is one way in which individuals who believe themselves to be unfairly treated can restore equity.

Such feelings of inequity may arise from a person paying far more in taxes than they receive in benefits (a comparison of what they give with what they receive) or from a comparison of one person's treatment with that of another.

For example, if a friend earns the same income as you but for some reason pays less tax, you may underdeclare income or make unwarranted deductions to make things fair. The survey evidence on whether tax evasion is associated with feelings of inequity is, however, equivocal. Spicer and Lundstedt (1976) and Wärneryd and Walerud (1982) found that self-reported evasion was correlated with perceived inequity. Spicer and Lundstedt surveyed 130 mainly middle- and higher-income households and investigated the relationship between a number of independent measures (e.g. perceived severity of sanctions, perceived inequity) and two dependent measures, a tax-resistance scale and a tax-evasion index. Perceived severity of sanctions did not correlate significantly with either of the dependent measures but those taxpayers who considered the exchange (tax paid and benefits received) with the government inequitable did show more tax resistance and scored higher on the evasion index. Similarly, Wärneryd and Walerud's telephone survey of over 400 men found that those agreeing with the statement 'The Swedish taxation system is unjust' and disagreeing with the statement 'Taking into consideration what the citizens get from the state, our taxes are not too high' were much more likely to admit evasion than those with opposite views. However, three larger surveys (also carried out in the United States and Sweden) have found no relationship (Mason & Calvin 1978; Laurin 1986; De Juan 1989). This may be due to differences in the wording of questions about fairness or to the masking of equity effects by other variables. Scott and Grasmick's (1981) results suggest that the latter is a plausible interpretation. They found that feelings of unfairness interacted with moral commitment and perceptions of sanctions to affect evasion. For those people who were inhibited from evading tax because they were worried about the consequences (in terms of guilt, stigma, or legal punishments) the relationship between perceived inequity and evasion was weak, whereas for the 'uninhibited' group there was a strong relationship.

In addition to the survey findings there is evidence from an experiment (Spicer & Becker 1980), and from studies using combined data on individuals (Elffers, Weigel & Hessing 1987) and at a macro level (Etzioni 1986). Spicer and Becker's study was described in chapter 2; to recapitulate briefly, they found that inequitable fiscal treatment to one's considerable disadvantage led to a higher percentage of taxes evaded and a favourable treatment had the opposite effect. The Elffers, Weigel, and Hessing study is more intriguing; they found that perceived inequity was significantly correlated with self-reported evasion but that the correlation with documented evasion was non-significant. This indirectly supports Wärneryd and Walerud's (1982) belief that perceived inequity is more likely to be an after-the-fact justification than a real motivation for evasion. Etzioni used survey data from 1960–80 and information on tax rates and estimates of tax evasion for that period to deduce that perceived inequity was associated with evasion since as the numbers of Americans perceiving taxes as fair declined so the numbers evading taxes increased.

We cannot draw firm conclusions from this mixed evidence. Feeling that the tax system is unfair is certainly associated with self-reported evasion for some groups but the causal relationship between these feelings and actual evasion is unclear. The subsequent experiments should shed some light on this.

3.1.2 *Social comparison and tax evasion*

Although the exchange relationship between taxpayer and the government can be seen as a simple dyad, in practice it is more complicated than this. Perceived inequity involves, at least in part, a comparison with others. Taxpayers make other comparisons: they may contrast their earnings with those of their friends, neighbours, and fellow workers and they may also compare their taxpaying behaviour with the same groups. In Benjamini and Maital's (1985) model the utility of evading is, indeed, partly a function of the size of the black economy, based on the notion that as the latter increases the stigma of evasion decreases. There is some evidence for this: Spicer and Lundstedt (1976), for example, have shown that self-reported tax evasion is positively related to the number of people one knows to have evaded taxes. But we know little about the psychological mechanisms that underlie these tax comparisons.

In this chapter, social comparison theory, specifically Rijsman's (1983) elaboration of Festinger's (1954) theory, was used to formulate hypotheses about tax-evasion behaviour. Essentially the idea was to see if a comparison of earnings would affect evasion. Now the evidence that level of earnings affects evasion is extremely mixed (Jackson & Milliron 1986) with researchers evenly divided between those who believe that people with high incomes evade more and those who believe the converse. It is possible that one reason for this confusion is that the important factor is not absolute income but relative income.

In the first experiment we manipulated earnings comparisons by giving people false feedback about the performance of other participants. Our simple-minded assumption was that those who were told they were performing relatively badly would be more likely to try to improve their position by evading tax. The other three experiments were based on Rijsman's (1983) social-competition theory. According to Rijsman, when people make comparisons they are motivated to discriminate themselves in a positive sense from their competitors. The consequences of such comparisons depend, however, on their nature: a comparison on an individual level leads to different changes in performance than one on a group or categorical level.

When people make comparisons on an individual level and discover that they are doing worse or as well as others, they will try to improve their performance. If they find that they are doing better than others they will make little effort to improve their performance. The idea behind this is that people seek to distinguish themselves from others. The same effects are not expected when people make comparisons on a group level. Those who discover that their social group is doing better than other social groups are expected to try even harder. The rationale for this is that 'the only way to build up . . . similarity with the status of the own category is to perform as the category does' (Rijsman 1983, 290–1). Whereas if you discover that your social group is doing the same or worse than other social groups the tendency to identify with your own group is weak or absent. In these cases there should be little attempt to improve performance.

If we make the reasonable assumption that evading tax is one way of improving financial performance, the relevance of Rijsman's theory is clear. Individuals who are told that they are earning less or the same as others should evade more tax than those who are told that they are earning more. People who are told that the social group to which they belong is earning more than other groups should try to earn more themselves. One way of earning more is to pay less tax.

3.1.3   *Individual differences in the predisposition to evade*
According to Jackson and Milliron (1986), the American IRS has identified sixty-four potential compliance factors ranging from variables such as income level and occupation to less obvious characteristics like intergenerational mobility (taxpayers with the same socio-economic background as their parents are thought to be more compliant than the upwardly or downwardly mobile). But, although individual differences are implicated in a number of the theories discussed in chapter 1 (e.g. Vogel 1974; Groenland & Van Veldhoven 1983; Weigel, Hessing & Elffers 1987), there has been little empirical work in this area apart from the common inclusion of demographic variables like age and sex. The consistent finding is that older people and women are more compliant and this seems to be true both in America (e.g. Mason & Calvin 1978) and Europe (e.g. Wärneryd & Walerud 1982; Van Eck & Kazemier 1988). A number of researchers have found no relationship between age or sex compliance but only rarely have reverse effects been found. As examples, Dornstein (1976) reported a positive relationship between age and noncompliance with bureaucratic tax rules among self-employed Israelis, and Friedland, Maital, and Rutenberg (1978) found that females evaded more than men in their experiment.

There have been both lifecycle and generational explanations for the age effect. It is possible that young people may be more willing to take risks and to admit illegal activities (behaviour which will change as they get older) or it could be that norms about taxpaying and evasion have altered over the years. There could be some truth in both of these explanations. To explore the age effect Mason and Lowry (1981) compared data from their 1975 and 1980 surveys and found that members of the 25–34 age group in 1980 were more compliant than the 21 to 24 age group in 1975. This supports a lifecycle-change explanation but the evidence is not compelling as the age intervals are different. Clotfelter's (1983) suggestion that there is a curvilinear relationship between age and compliance with the oldest and youngest individuals being the most compliant is intriguing, but to date his study provides the only evidence for this.

In Jackson and Milliron's (1986) comprehensive review, personality variables are included under the heading 'other variables' along with a very mixed bag of factors like race, religion and party affiliation. This is rather surprising since there are good reasons for supposing that 'core' attitudes and personality variables will be related to evasion. To take just one example, Neal and Rettig (1967) have argued that a sense of alienation increases the probability of deviance as personal constraints about the propriety of one's actions are minimised. Evasion is a form of deviance and we might therefore expect alienation to increase the propensity to evade. Another and more specific example is Groenland and Van Veldhoven's (1983) hypothesis that people with an internal locus of control (those who see their environment as largely under their personal control) will succeed in evading taxes more often than those with an external locus of control. The rationale for this is that internals are thought to make better use of information generally and an expectation that they will be more alert to new evasion opportunities.

Groenland and Van Veldhoven's study provides some support for their hypotheses, in that there was an interaction between level of education and locus of control. Among the better educated, internals did, indeed, evade more; this relationship was reversed for those with a lower education. In a follow-up study, however, Groenland and Van Zon (1984) failed to replicate this and also failed to find the expected relationship between alienation and evasion (though De Juan (1989) reports that alienation played a significant role in predicting tax attitudes, which in turn predicted propensity to evade).

Our initial interest in exploring individual differences and evasion grew out of a desire to test out the ecological validity of tax-evasion experiments. Elffers, Weigel, and Hessing (1987) used a wide variety of measures of attitudes, subjective norms and 'core' attitudes and found that the pattern of predictors for self-reported evasion and documented evasion was different. Only 'core' attitude measures (alienation, tolerance of illegal behaviour, competitive orientation) correlated with documented evasion. Attitudes and social norms, on the other hand, were associated with self-reported evasion.

Knowing what predicts experimental evasion would clearly help place this behaviour. Thus in the final two studies in the chapter a selection of the Elffers, Weigel, and Hessing variables were used.

3.2   UK05: The effect of inequity and earnings comparisons on evasion

Method

Subjects   Fifty-four first-year undergraduate students took part, recruited from the department's subject pool. Fourteen of these were psychology students. Most were recruited through a letter which stated, in part, that 'this letter is not actively a request for subjects in a psychology experiment, but rather an offer for you to take part in a small-business simulation'.

Design   Two variables were investigated: equity (three levels) and earnings comparison (three levels). Equity was manipulated by simply altering the information about taxation to 'Your tax rate is 30% and the average tax rate is x.' The value of x depended on which condition the subject was in. To induce perceptions of inequity, one third of the subjects were told that the tax rate was 15%, one third that it was 45%, and the remainder that it was 30%. Earnings comparison was manipulated by providing participants with false feedback at the end of the first year. At the outset they were told that 'Your performance will be compared with that of your competitors (all other participants in this simulation). At the conclusion of the simulation a money reward will be distributed according to your performance in terms of net income accumulated.' Subsequently, at the end of the first year, one third of the subjects were told that their competitors were, on average, more successful than them, one third that their competitors were, on average, less successful than them, and the remainder that they were as successful.

Procedure   This was based on that used for UK04, though a number of modifications were made to the program and subjects were tested in many batches. The changes were made to incorporate the two manipulations of interest (equity and social comparison) and to try and ensure that participants perceived the simulation as a serious task in which the focus was on managing a business, and not as a game or a psychology experiment.

The task-related changes were not extensive but were important. First, subjects were given a written copy of the initial instructions that appeared on the screen so that they could refer to them during the simulation. Second, the study was presented as a management investigation that was only incidentally being carried out in the psychology department. To this end the initial screen display was a title page in stylish graphics which said: SMALL-BUSINESS SIMULATION, copyright Business Research Associates 1984, and the opening sentence of the instructions was altered to 'This is a simulation produced by Business Research Associates to investigate behaviour in small businesses.'

Table 3.1. *Mean percentage of income not declared as a function of equity and comparison condition (N = 54)*

	Equity condition									
	Overtaxed			Equitable			Undertaxed			
Year	1	2	Average	1	2	Average	1	2	Average	Overall
Comparison condition										
Competitors are:										
More successful	7	12	10	24	35	30	14	40	27	22
As successful	3	14	9	9	18	14	2	7	5	9
Less successful	12	21	17	6	0	3	19	18	17	13
Overall	7	16	12	13	18	16	12	22	17	15

The aim of each participant was also redefined as 'managing your business as successfully as possible'. Finally the tax-man graphics were removed.

To simplify the task all participants were told that the audit rate was 1 in 6 and the fine rate 6 times the amount of tax evaded. In fact, one third were audited once, one third twice and one third on three occasions. This was predetermined and controlled across conditions.

Results

The data were analysed using two $2 \times 3 \times 3$ partially repeated measures analyses of variance, with equity (3 levels) and earnings comparison (3 levels) as between-groups factors and year (first or second) as a within-group factor. For the percentage of income declared there was a significant difference between the first and second year overall ($F = 5.4$, $df = 1,45$, $p < 0.05$) and the interaction between earnings comparison and year approached significance ($F = 3.0$, $df = 2,45$, $p < 0.1$). None of the other effects were significant. As Table 3.1 shows, overall less income was declared in year two than year one, though this was not true for the group who were told that their competitors were less successful than them.

The pattern of results for the frequency of underdeclaring was very similar though none of the effects were significant. The main effect of earnings comparison and the interaction between earnings comparison and year approached significance ($F = 2.4$, $df = 2,45$, $p < 0.1$: $F = 2.7$, $df = 2,45$, $p < 0.1$). As Table 3.2 shows, income was more often underdeclared when competitors were more successful and this effect was more pronounced in the second year. There was no effect of being audited on the number of periods that income was underdeclared.

Table 3.2. *Mean number of periods (out of 12) that income was
underdeclared as a function of equity and comparison condition (N = 54)*

	Equity condition									
	Overtaxed			Equitable			Undertaxed			
Year	1	2	Average	1	2	Average	1	2	Average	Overall
Comparison condition										
Competitors are:										
More successful	3.5	4.0	3.8	2.5	3.7	3.1	3.7	4.8	4.3	3.7
As successful	1.7	2.5	2.1	2.8	3.0	2.9	1.2	2.3	1.8	2.3
Less successful	2.7	2.5	2.6	2.5	1.8	2.2	2.7	2.7	2.7	2.5
Overall	2.6	3.0	2.9	2.6	2.8	2.7	2.5	3.3	2.9	2.8

Discussion

These results show that, contrary to Spicer and Becker's (1980) findings, equity did not have a significant effect on tax evasion; indeed it barely had any effect at all on either the percentage of income declared or the frequency of underdeclaring. There are at least three possible reasons for this. First, in Spicer and Becker's study there was a 25% difference between the tax rate of the inequity groups and the average tax rate, whereas in our study, in order to use more realistic tax rates, the difference was only 15%. This lessens the strength of the equity manipulation. Second, Spicer and Becker's subjects were told that they were taking part in a 'tax game or simulation' and had little information other than that about tax rates. The demand characteristics of the task in their study must have been very apparent to the participants. In contrast, here the details about own and average tax rates were just part of the initial instructions, and it is possible that this information was ignored or forgotten. To check this out a letter was sent to all participants at the beginning of the next term (six weeks after the final batch of subjects had been run) giving them some information about collecting their prizes and also asking them to answer two questions about their own and the average tax rate. Unfortunately only 19 responses were obtained. Of these 8 correctly identified the relative status of their tax rate, 4 couldn't remember at all, and 7 misidentified their position, claiming in 5 cases that the average tax rate was the same as their own and in the other 2 that it was less. This provides some very weak evidence that the equity manipulation was attended to. Third, it is possible that feelings of inequity are, as both Wärneryd and Walerud (1982) and De Juan (1989) have suggested, rationalisations of inequity rather than determinants of it.

There is some evidence, though it is not compelling, that giving subjects information about their competitors' performance affected evasion. When subjects were told that their competitors were more or as successful at the end of year one, they evaded tax more often and declared less income during year two. When subjects were told that their competitors were less successful they essentially behaved the same way in year two as they had in year one. This is exactly the pattern that Rijsman (1983) would predict for comparisons on an individual level.

The results revealed an unexpected overall effect of year. A lower percentage of income was declared in the second year. There seem to be two likely explanations for this effect. It could be that subjects take time fully to understand the task and realise that tax evasion is a possibility. However, *t*-tests comparing the first three and last three periods of the first year revealed no significant differences. An alternative is that in the last few periods of the second year, subjects take greater risks in order to gain an advantage over their competitors. However, *t*-tests comparing the first three and the last three periods of the second year also showed no significant effects. It must be noted that these comparisons were possible for only thirty-seven subjects as some raw data files stored on magnetic tape were corrupt.

3.3   UK06: Effects of social comparison and inequity on evasion

In this study we used a more sophisticated form of social comparison and a different equity manipulation. Rather than a simple comparison with other participants, subjects either made personal or categorical level comparisons. The equity manipulation was altered to make it more plausible and more salient.

Method

Subjects Forty-eight members of the general public (24 men and 24 women) were recruited by confederates. The modal net income of the subjects was between £7,000 and £8,000. Subjects were tested in batches, one or two at a time, at various off-campus locations (private homes, local museum). All subjects received refreshment and an honorarium of £1.

Design Four variables were investigated: equity (three levels), social-comparison type (personal, categorical), nature of comparison (equal, superior), and when audits occurred (periods 1, 4, 7, or 11). The dependent measures were the overall percentage of income declared and the number of periods in which income was underdeclared.

Subjects were told that they would all receive a tax-free starter's allowance of £2,200. However, in the negative inequity condition they were told that the average allowance was £3,600, in the equity condition that the average allowance was the same as theirs, and in the positive inequity condition that the average allowance was £800. To increase the salience of this manipulation, the allowance was continued in the second and third years at a reduced level (£1,100 and £550) but without a change in its percentage of the stated average allowance, which was also reduced.

In the personal social-comparison conditions, participants were told that their performance would be compared with that of their direct competitor, *Paul's*. In the categorical social-comparison conditions the performance of the cooperative that individuals were members of was compared with that of another cooperative. These comparisons were fictitious. Participants were told that they had performed either as well as or better than the person/group with which they were being compared.

Subjects were informed that audits would take place randomly, but no information was given about the frequency of audits. Each subject was audited once. Audits took place either in the 1st, 4th, 7th or 11th period (of 12 consecutive periods).

Procedure   The first part of the study consisted of the shop simulation, which on average took about forty minutes. Subjects subsequently completed two brief questionnaires, which included questions on personal information (age, sex, marital status, employment status, income, educational level) and manipulation checks (some were factual, e.g. 'with whom were you compared during the simulation?', and some asked about personal feelings, e.g. 'how much value did you attach to the fact that your performance was compared with that of another shopkeeper?').

After some introductory information on how to operate the computer, subjects read the following instructions from the screen (they were also given a written version for reference).

> This is a simulation produced by Robben's Business Research to investigate behaviour in small businesses. You are to imagine that you set yourself up as a shopkeeper. You will have to make a series of decisions over a three-year period. For example, you will have to decide about the selling price of your products (soft-drinks and spirits), whether you want to buy any additional information, and whether to advertise or not. You will also have to report your income and pay tax on the amount reported. As a governmental subsidy, you will receive a tax-free starter's allowance of £2,200 in the first year of your business. Every participant will receive an allowance, which is on average £x [the value of x varied according to condition].
>
> Your purpose in this simulation is to manage your business as successfully as possible.
>
> Your performance will be compared with that of your direct competitor called *Paul's*. The owner of that shop is in fact another participant in this

simulation. The data of this person were collected on an earlier occasion. All the relevant data are stored in this computer so they can easily be compared with yours. [In the categorical comparison condition this paragraph referred to cooperatives.]

Each year is divided into four quarters: Spring, Summer, Autumn and Winter. Each quarter you will be asked to do four things. These are:
1. decide whether or not you want to buy information, and if so, what kind
2. decide whether or not you want to advertise for that quarter, and if so, how much you will spend
3. set your prices for the products you sell in that quarter
4. make a tax return.

INFORMATION

Information is of six kinds and costs £50 per bit. You may buy only one bit of information per quarter. The following information is available:
1. market research on consumers
2. forecasts of likely tax changes
3. forecasts of trends in the market
4. agency research on the effectiveness of advertising
5. research on the seasonal effects of sales
6. pricing in the retail business.

ADVERTISING

Advertising costs £100 per unit. You may buy up to five units per quarter.

PRICES

You may charge any price per product that you wish, but at high prices you will get too little custom, and at low prices you cannot cope with the demand. In line with this, we have set a minimum and maximum price for each product. Your selling price has to be set within that range.

TAXATION

At the end of each quarter your total receipts will be calculated. You will be asked to report your taxable income for that quarter (receipts minus advertising and information costs). The tax rate during the simulation will be 35%. From time to time, audits will be conducted according to a random sample. If you are drawn in the random sample then you will be audited. If you underreported income then, for this period only, you will have to pay the amount of tax due plus a penalty. The maximum penalty is completely up to the discretion of the tax inspector.

The simulation is about to start. For your convenience, we summarise the different decisions you have to make in each quarter.

First, you have to decide whether you want to buy information.

Second, you have to decide whether you want to advertise or not.

> Third, you have to set your selling prices.
> Fourth, you will be asked to make a tax return.
>
> Your can always refer to the written instructions if you need to.

In each period subjects would be asked to make the four decisions mentioned above. For example, in the first period a subject might pay for information about the effectiveness of advertising, and would then see this:

> ADVERTISING EFFECTIVENESS
> According to Grieveson-Bennet, a local advertising agency, the market for a shop like yours is significantly affected by advertising. They reckon that each unit of advertising bought will increase sales by 5%. However, they point out that this is only true up to a certain amount of advertising. Above that amount, the increase of sales will be less than 5% for each unit of advertising.

They might then decide to buy 5 units of advertising (at £80 a unit) and would then see this:

Product line	Average wholesale price	Set your selling price
Soft drinks	£0.15	£0.30
Spirits	£4.00	£7.00

Having set the price for soft drinks as 30p and spirits as £7, the following would then be displayed on the screen:

> These are the results of your sales in the spring of year 1:

Product line	Your profit per item	Items sold	Profits
Soft drinks	£0.15	18,041	£2,706.15
Spirits	£3.00	941	£2,823.00

And, after a short pause, this:

> It is year 1, spring.
> Your balance sheet this spring is as follows:

Total profits	£5,529.15
Advertising costs	£400.00
Information costs	£50.00
Taxable income	£5,079.15

> How much of your TAXABLE INCOME do you want to declare?

After the subjects had made their income declaration, there was a pause. Subjects were then informed whether they had been audited or not, their gross income, net income and total fines to date displayed, and then the next period began.

Results

The data were analysed using two three-way analyses of variance. For the

Table 3.3. *Mean number of times (out of 12) that income was underdeclared as a function of equity and social comparison (N=48)*

	Equity condition			
	Negative	Neutral	Positive	Overall
Personal social comparison				
Equal	7.5	8.8	2.8	6.3
Superior	9.0	8.5	2.3	6.6
Average	8.3	8.6	2.5	6.5
Categorical social comparison				
Equal	7.0	7.3	9.0	7.8
Superior	3.0	3.8	5.3	4.0
Average	5.0	5.5	7.1	5.9

Table 3.4. *Mean percentage of income not declared as a function of equity and social comparison (N=48)*

	Equity condition			
	Negative	Neutral	Positive	Overall
Personal social comparison				
Equal	14	27	4	15
Superior	42	32	3	26
Average	28	30	4	20
Categorical social comparison				
Equal	23	22	17	21
Superior	5	4	8	6
Average	14	13	13	13

percentage of income declared there were no significant effects. For frequency of underdeclaring the interaction between equity condition and type of comparison (personal, categorical) came close to significance ($F = 3.0$, $df = 2,36$, critical value of $F = 3.3$) (see Table 3.3). Overall, subjects who performed equally well as their competitors evaded taxes on more occasions than those whose performance was superior. In the positive inequity condition, evasion was least frequent, and highest in the neutral condition. Table 3.3 shows that the picture is more complicated when separating the effects for the experimental cells.

The percentage of income not reported was very similar for both comparison conditions (see Table 3.4). It was lowest for the positive inequity

Table 3.5. *Mean number of times (out of 4) that income was underdeclared as a function of year and audit occurrence (N=48)*

	Period in which audit occurred				
	1	4	7	11	Average
Year					
1	1.3	2.3	2.1	2.1	1.9
2	0.8	2.2	2.8	2.4	2.2
3	1.0	2.2	2.9	2.3	2.1
Average	1.0	2.2	2.6	2.3	2.1

condition and highest for the neutral and negative inequity condition. Again, the picture appears more complicated when taking a look at the different experimental cells.

To explore the effects of being audited, pre- and post-audit income declarations were compared using *t*-tests. No significant differences were found. A 2 × 3 × 4 partially repeated measures analysis of variance with type of comparison (2 levels) and audit occurrence (4 levels) as between-groups factors and year (3 levels) as a within-groups factor found no significant effects for frequency of underdeclaring, although being audited in year 1 did appear to result in less evasion (see Table 3.5). The number of occasions on which not all income was reported did not differ much between the years, although it was highest in year 2. When audited after the very first period of the simulation, the frequency of evasion was clearly the least.

Discussion

The results of this experiment suggest that feelings of inequity may not affect tax evasion and are in line with the results of UK05. Both studies are compatible with the large-scale survey studies of Laurin (1986), Mason and Calvin (1978), and De Juan (1989). Although we are unhappy about arguing from null results, on balance we find this reassuring. People probably do sometimes use unfairness of the tax system as a justification for evasion. This is congruent with what we know about the use of justifications in general (Tedeschi & Reiss 1981) and fits Elffers, Weigel, and Hessing's (1987) finding that equity was correlated only with self-reported evasion and not documented evasion. Perceived inequity probably does not, however, play a causal role. Hedging our conclusions with 'probably' is not just academic caution. There is a serious worry that part of the reason for failing to find an effect of equity may be due to the difficulty of inducing feelings of inequity experimentally. Only ten subjects reported noticing a difference between their allowance and the average allowance and most subjects said they paid little attention to the information about allowances. The equity variable was not salient enough.

Social comparison had no significant effect and in fact the results were in the opposite direction to those predicted: in the personal social comparison condition those told that they were doing better than others evaded more and in the categorical social condition those told that their cooperative were doing better evaded less. This is hard to attribute to weak manipulations: in the postexperimental questionnaire all but two subjects stated the comparison object correctly although most indicated that the comparison of their performance with others was of only slight importance to them. Subjects rated the importance of the fact that their performance was compared with another shopkeeper/cooperative on a 5-point scale ($1 =$ no importance, $5 =$ very important) and the mean rating was 2.54. Some however did say that the comparison evoked competitive feelings.

The more important aspect of this study was probably that it was carried out on a nonstudent sample and so paved the way to the next study, which examined social comparison in more detail and looked at individual differences and the ecological validity of experimental studies of evasion.

3.4 UK07: Social comparison and correlates of evasion

Method

Subjects A total of 41 men and 31 women took part. A leaflet was distributed in a middle-class residential area inviting participation in a study of small-business behaviour. This was followed up by door-to-door canvassing. A wide range of occupations was represented: teachers, housewives, accountants, businessmen, bankers, policemen, and one tax inspector. Subjects were tested individually in a room in a University Hall of Residence. Subjects were rewarded by a bottle of wine distributed some months after the study had been completed.

Design Two variables were investigated experimentally: social comparison type (personal, categorical) and nature of the comparison (inferior, equal, superior). In addition, questionnaires based on those used by Elffers, Weigel, and Hessing (1987) were sent out some months after the experiment had been completed to obtain attitude, social norm, and personality measures.

Procedure The computer simulation was very similar to that used in UK06 with the addition of an inferior social comparison condition. Instead of administering postexperimental questionnaires, all subjects were interviewed in an open-ended way about the experiment. The attitude, social norm, and personality questionnaire was sent to all 72 subjects – 65 returned

completed questionnaires, a response rate of 90%. The questionnaire was
split into three parts. The first combined a measure of alienation based on
Srole's (1956) scale (e.g. 'Most people really don't care what happens to the
next fellow') with ten items drawn from Rundquist and Sletto's (1936)
measure of attitudes towards the law (e.g. 'Court decisions are almost always
just'). The nineteen statements were presented in a strongly agree/strongly
disagree format with five response categories. The second comprised three
words/phrases which had to be rated on five bipolar adjectives drawn from
the evaluative factor of the semantic differential (good/bad, pleasant/
unpleasant, honest/dishonest, blameworthy/not blameworthy, kind/
unkind). The words/phrases were 'competition', 'making false deductions on a tax return', and 'concealing income on a tax return'. The final part
measured self-reported tax evasion ('Did you, when filling in your 1983/4
tax form understate your income or report any unwarranted deductions?')
and perceived social support for tax evasion ('How do you think other people
near to you would react if you were to evade taxes?').

Results
The data from the simulation were analysed using a $2 \times 3 \times 3$ partially
repeated measures analysis of variance with type of comparison (2 types),
nature of comparison (3 levels) as between-groups factors and year (1, 2, or
3) as a within-groups factor. Neither for the percentage of income underdeclared nor for the frequency of underdeclaring were there any significant
results (see Table 3.6). A one-way analysis of variance of audit showed no
significant effects on the behaviour; also, subjects audited in period 1 did not
act differently from those audited in other periods.
    The data from the questionnaires were more rewarding. Table 3.7 shows
the correlations between the various measures and frequency of underreporting during the simulation. Two of the 'central' attitudes measures were
significantly correlated with simulated evasion. Only five individuals reported evading tax in either or both of the two previous years, so no
correlations with self-reported tax evasion are shown.

Discussion
Although the results from the simulation were nonsignificant, the pattern of
results for the equal and superior conditions is very similar to those of UK06.
Taking the personal comparison condition alone, the results are similar to
UK05, in that there the effect was for those in the 'inferior' condition to evade
more. This suggests that a larger study might be able to demonstrate that
social comparison has an effect although hardly one that Rijsman's (1983)
theory would predict.
    It was notable that the level of evasion in this and the previous study was

Table 3.6. *Mean number of times (out of 12) that income was underdeclared and percentage of income not reported (in brackets) as a function of type and nature of social comparison (N = 72)*

| | Nature of comparison | | | |
	Inferior	Equal	Superior	Overall
Personal social comparison	6.2 (13.2)	2.1 (3.8)	3.3 (6.9)	3.8 (6.7)
Categorical social comparison	2.8 (2.4)	4.3 (14.4)	2.3 (2.4)	3.1 (6.4)
Overall	4.5 (7.8)	3.2 (9.1)	2.8 (4.7)	3.5 (6.6)

Table 3.7. *Correlations between tax evasion during the simulation and measures of attitudes, subjective norms and central attitudes (N = 65)*

	Frequency of underreporting
Attitudes	
Underreporting income	0.05
False deductions	0.10
Subjective norms	
Social support	0.23
Central attitudes	
Alienation	0.28*
Attitude towards law	−0.26*
Competitiveness	−0.11

*$p < 0.05$

much lower than in previous experiments (43 of the 72 subjects were completely honest). This is probably due to the fact that the tax declaration was embedded in a shop simulation (and so the purpose of the experiment was not obvious) and a consequence of using members of the general public as subjects. Members of the general public may well take fewer risks than students and also take the study more seriously.

That the measures which predict tax evasion in the simulation are similar to those found to predict documented tax evasion was encouraging and lent credence to experimental studies. The one 'central' attitude which did not correlate significantly was ratings of 'competition'. Respondents found this section of the questionnaire the most difficult to fill in, and many complained about the instructions for this part. So the lack of significance here is perhaps understandable. Rather more difficult to explain is that 'social support' is correlated with experimental evasion. Elffers, Weigel, and Hessing found that this variable correlated with self-reported evasion but not with documented evasion. This needs further investigation.

3.5   NL01: Social comparison and correlates of evasion

Method

This study is a replication of UK07.

Subjects   A random sample from the local telephone directory was made of telephone numbers starting with a preselected code. Then a letter was sent inviting the recipient (or one of his or her family members over 21 with job experience) to participate in an economic-behaviour research project involving microcomputers. A few days after this mailing the recipients were contacted by telephone and asked personally whether they were interested in taking part. Of 291 persons contacted, 22 women and 50 men agreed to participate, a response rate of just under 25%. The subjects were aged between 21 and 71, with an average of 40 years. All subjects were tested individually.

Design   Three between-groups factors were employed in the study: type of comparison (individual, categorical), nature of comparison (inferior, similar, superior), and period in which the tax return was audited. The first factor was manipulated by informing subjects that their business results were to be compared with those of another *individual* subject, or by telling subjects they were allocated to a *cooperative* of shopkeepers, whose results would be compared with those of another cooperative. Subjects were led to believe that the comparison thus was to be made on an individual performance level or a collective performance level.

The second factor was manipulated by informing subjects that their performance was either inferior, similar, or superior to their competitors' performance. The performance of the subject in terms of net income was explicitly presented at the end of each period and at the end of each year. In the latter case, a statement about the subject's position relative to the comparison other/s was made. This information about relative performance was independent of subjects' actual performance and was stable across the years, i.e. subjects always received information pertaining to their initial relative position.

During the simulation, each subject was audited once; the audit occurred either in the first, fourth, seventh or eleventh period.

The dependent measures were (a) the overall frequency of underdeclaring and the overall percentage of income declared and (b) the frequency of underdeclaring and the percentage of income declared in each of the three years of the simulation (there were four periods per year).

Procedure   The study was divided into two parts, the first being the shop simulation and the second involving completing a questionnaire measuring sociodemographics, attitudes, norms, perceptions, personality attributes, and risk-taking behaviour. Both parts took, on average, about a similar amount of time to complete for the subjects and 83 minutes in all.

The shop simulation was the same as in UK07 with the text carefully translated into Dutch. After some information on how to operate the computer the subjects read, from the computer screen, instructions about the shop simulation.

People were instructed to act as *they themselves* saw fit under the circumstances, and to try to run their businesses as successfully as possible.

The questionnaire measured a variety of relevant variables. Attitudes towards underreporting income and towards claiming unwarranted deductions were measured using semantic differentials (as in Elffers, Weigel & Hessing 1987). Rather than the Srole (1956) scale used in UK07, alienation was assessed using a Dutch translation of Zeller, Neal, and Groat's (1980) scale. This has four subscales which cover social isolation, powerlessness, normlessness, and meaninglessness. Disinhibition was measured using Hauber, Toornvliet, and Willemse's (1986) scale. This is based on Zuckerman's (1979) sensation-seeking scale and is concerned with the need for excitement derived in an unconventional way (e.g. a frequent use of alcohol and drugs, a liberal sexual morality, non-conformist style of life). Social support was measured by one item which asked how people in the everyday environment would react to the respondents' possible tax-evasion behaviour and social orientation by a Decomposed Games instrument containing 32 self–other money allocations (Liebrand 1982). This instrument required the subject to choose between two stimuli for 32 times. Each stimulus represented a distribution of (imaginary) money between oneself and a hypothetical other. For instance, stimulus A could distribute an amount of $+f15$ to oneself, and $-f5$ to the other; stimulus B would then provide a different distribution. According to the scores on this instrument, subjects were classified as altruistic, cooperative, individualistic, or competitive.

Subjects received a bottle of red wine for their participation in the simulation study. For completing the questionnaire they were given a choice between a lottery ticket with a chance of 1 in 100 of winning 100 guilders, or a ticket with a chance of 1 in 25 of winning 25 guilders, or an unconditional reward of 2.50 guilders (just under £1). This choice constituted a measure of behavioural risk-taking by the subjects. Prizes were paid immediately in cash or transferred by bank.

Results

Simulation data First, the data obtained in the simulation were analysed using $2 \times 3 \times 4$ analyses of variance with type of comparison (individual, categorical), nature of comparison (inferior, similar, superior), and period

Table 3.8. *Mean number of times (out of 12) that income was underdeclared and percentage of income not reported (in brackets) as a function of nature and type of comparison and the audit variable ($N = 72$)*

	Period in which audit occurred				
	1	4	7	11	Overall
Nature of comparison					
Inferior	5.3 (8.9)	5.8 (6.1)	5.8 (16.5)	6.5 (19.5)	5.9 (12.8)
Similar	1.5 (2.6)	7.0 (10.4)	5.7 (7.4)	5.5 (8.0)	4.9 (7.1)
Superior	11.0 (29.2)	2.0 (8.6)	10.2 (38.6)	5.3 (11.5)	7.1 (22.0)
Overall	5.9 (13.6)	4.9 (8.4)	7.2 (20.9)	5.8 (13.0)	6.0 (13.9)
Type of comparison					
Personal	4.2 (8.9)	7.4 (14.2)	7.3 (34.0)	5.6 (8.7)	6.1 (16.5)
Categorical	7.7 (18.2)	2.6 (2.5)	7.1 (7.7)	6.0 (17.3)	5.8 (11.4)
Average	5.9 (13.6)	5.0 (8.4)	7.2 (20.9)	5.8 (13.0)	6.0 (13.9)

in which the audit occurred as between-groups factors and the overall frequency of underdeclaring and overall percentage of income declared as dependent measures. The effect of nature of comparison approached significance for the percentage of income declared ($F = 2.9$, $df = 2,48$, $p < 0.063$).

A significant interaction was found between nature of comparison and the audit variable for frequency of underdeclaring ($F = 2.7$, $df = 6,48$, $p < 0.05$). This interaction indicates that those in the superior-performance condition generally evaded on more occasions than those in the other conditions, but showed a sharp decrease in the frequency of evasion for those audited in the 4th period (upper part of Table 3.8).

Questionnaire data   Table 3.9 shows the significant correlations between the various measures and tax evasion. As expected, older participants evaded less. Attitudes towards not reporting income and towards claiming unwarranted deductions, a strong sense of alienation, a self-serving rather than community-directed orientation, and a tendency to express oneself with socially proscribed behaviours were all positively associated with frequency of underdeclaring. The percentage of income not declared was correlated with the alienation and the self-serving orientation measures.

The behavioural risk measure showed a virtual zero correlation with tax evasion in the experiment: 5 people chose the immediate cash reward, 25 went for the 1-in-25 chance to win 25 guilders, and 42 opted for the 1-in-100 chance to win 100 guilders, indicating a negative risk premium.

Table 3.9. *Correlations between experimental tax-evasion behaviour and personal characteristics (N = 72)*

	Frequency	Percentage not reported
Attitudes		
Underreporting[1]	0.37	0.05
Unwarranted deductions[1]	0.30	0.04
Subjective norms		
Social support	0.18	0.02
Central attitudes		
Alienation[1]	0.46	0.25
Disinhibition[1]	0.29	0.13
Competitiveness[1]	0.27	0.29
Social orientation[1]	0.27	0.30
Demographics		
Age[2]	−0.21	−0.05
Employment status[3]	−0.23	−0.01
Sex[4]	0.07	−0.03

Note: Correlations over 0.20 are at least significant at $p = 0.05$
[1] A high score indicates a stronger presence of that characteristic
[2] In years
[3] 1 = having a job, 2 = without a job
[4] 1 = female, 2 = male

Cross-national comparisons   The experimental results of this study can be compared to those of UK07 as the simulation is an exact replication. There is a striking difference in evasion between the samples. In the Dutch sample far more evaders were present than in the British sample: 52 out of 72 participants evaded at least once compared to 30 out of 72 in the British sample ($\chi^2 = 12.5$, $df = 1$, $p < 0.001$). This is puzzling. Frey and Weck (1987) claim that evasion should be higher in the Netherlands than in Britain if factors such as the size of the tax burden are relevant, but there is actually no evidence that this is so. Given that our subsequent cross-national studies do not show this large difference it seems unlikely that it is caused by existing differences in everyday evasion. The pattern of results does not correspond at all (see Table 3.10).

The present data can also be compared with questionnaire data from UK07 and the findings of Elffers, Weigel, and Hessing (1987) (Table 3.11). Unlike the Elffers, Weigel, and Hessing and the UK07 studies, attitudes towards evading taxes by underreporting income and by overstating deductions correlated significantly with the number of periods in which tax was evaded. In the UK07 study competitiveness (self-serving orientation) was not positively related to tax-evasion behaviour, whereas in this study it is, in accordance with the Weigel, Hessing, and Elffers (1987) model.

Table 3.10. *Mean number of times (out of 12) that income was underdeclared as a function of type and nature of social comparison (N = 72 for each sample)*

	Nature of comparison			
	Inferior	Equal	Superior	Average
Personal social comparison	5.3 (6.2)	5.6 (2.1)	7.5 (3.3)	6.1 (3.9)
Categorical social comparison	6.4 (2.8)	4.3 (4.3)	6.8 (2.3)	5.8 (3.1)
Average	5.9 (4.5)	4.9 (3.2)	7.1 (2.8)	6.0 (3.5)

Note: UK figures given in brackets

Table 3.11. *Comparison of results obtained in UK07, NL01, and Elffers, Weigel, and Hessing (1987): correlations between attitudes, subjective norms, personality attributes and tax-evasion behaviour (N's are 72, 72, and 155, respectively)*

	UK07	NL01	Elffers, Weigel, and Hessing	
			Documented status	Self-reported status
Attitudes				
Underreporting income	n.s.	0.37	n.s.	0.25
False deductions	n.s.	0.30	n.s.	0.19
Subjective norms				
Social support	n.s.	n.s.	n.s.	0.22
Personality attributes				
Alienation	0.28	0.46	0.22	n.s.
Social orientation	n.s.	0.27	0.17	n.s.
Competitiveness	—	0.27	0.17	n.s.
Attitude towards law	−0.26	—	−0.18	n.s.

—: no information

Discussion

As in previous experiments in which the effects of social comparison on tax-evasion behaviour were investigated, no significant results were obtained (UK05, UK06, UK07) for any of the measures of tax evasion. One reason for this may be that the subjects clearly were not aware of the real (and hidden) meaning of the experiment. Research by Rijsman (1974, 1983) has shown that the predicted effects are obtained when the comparison dimension is made explicit to the subjects and, for obvious reasons, in this study tax evasion is not made salient to the subjects. However, on the dimension they thought they were compared on (final net income), there were also no effects of social comparison although subjects were explicitly informed about their relative position. It thus appears that the social comparison variables did not motivate subjects to change their financial and tax-evasion behaviours.

From Table 3.9 we see that the decision to evade taxes (as represented by the frequency variable) and the magnitude of tax evasion (as represented by the percentage variable) are clearly distinct in that they are related to different demographic and personality variables. Only the alienation and self-serving orientation measures seem to form shared influencing parameters. The results suggest that people who are not society oriented, young, with a job, and with positive attitudes towards the behaviour are most likely to be associated with tax-evasion behaviour. In contrast with other tax-evasion experiments (Spicer & Becker 1980; Spicer & Hero 1985) no effect of sex was found on either the decision to evade taxes or the size of the misrepresentation of income.

By contrasting the present results with those obtained in research on documented tax-evasion behaviour, one can get some idea of how well the experimental data match the pattern of variables that have been useful in explaining real behaviour. In UK07 we reported a similar comparison which generally supported the model delineated by Weigel, Hessing, and Elffers (1987). The UK07 and Elffers, Weigel, and Hessing studies indicated that the personality variables represented the strongest correlates of tax-evasion behaviour, with attitudinal variables being of little importance. In this study, on the other hand, attitudes towards evading tax correlated significantly with tax-evasion behaviour. A possible explanation might be that in the present study, unlike the earlier ones, tax-evasion behaviour and attitudes towards that behaviour were measured within a short time of each other. This may have made it more likely that subjects would answer the attitude items so that they would be congruent with their behaviour.

3.6 Conclusions

Unfortunately from the work reported in this chapter we cannot tell a clear and simple story. On the one hand, that alienation, social orientation, and competitiveness all correlate with evasion during an experiment is extremely encouraging: it fits the theoretical model of Weigel, Hessing, and Elffers (1987) as well as other models which emphasise the role of individual differences, and enables us to locate our measure of evasion within the universe of such measures. Out of admitted evasion, self-reported audit outcome and officially documented evasion, the kind of noncompliance found in the experiments corresponds most closely to the last two. On the other hand, the evidence we have produced on the role of equity and social comparison is disappointing in the extreme. As we have already discussed, it is possible that equity is not, after all, a particularly important variable. But we retain a residual belief, despite all the evidence, that earnings comparisons and relative income are probably relevant for certain social groups. This belief cannot be justified by any of the evidence presented earlier, since we have found it impossible to discern any pattern in the results of the four studies, but we retain it none the less.

It is appropriate to make two further points, one about the experimental methodology, the other about cross-national comparisons. Webley and Halstead (1986) concluded that for experiments 'to make a significant contribution to our understanding of tax evasion they must be considerably more sophisticated'. The experiments reported in this chapter are certainly an improvement in methodological terms on earlier studies although those can clearly be refined: for example the dependent measures in all four studies were based on a repetitious series of income declarations and there are good reasons for allowing participants to make different kinds of income declarations (e.g. income from investment as well as income from earnings) and claim for allowable deductions. Dependent measures based on income declarations are not a poor measure of compliance; after all, underdeclaring income is apparently a more popular form of evasion than overclaiming allowances (Kinsey 1984). But it is possible that altering a business expense may be seen in a different light to underdeclaring income, and participants in experiments should be able to evade in as many ways as they can in everyday life.

Cross-national investigations may be carried out to exploit naturally occurring differences in independent measures, such as differences in 'tax mentality' and tax rates, or to ascertain the extent to which theories and findings are general or confined to specific socio-cultural settings. Our cross-national studies are of the second type; we are trying to demonstrate that equity, social comparison, and, in the next chapter, withholding and opportunity, are relevant regardless of the idiosyncratic features of tax (and other) systems. The cross-national comparisons in this chapter cannot be said to have been particularly successful; the independent variables had no effect in either country and there was an unexpected difference in the amount of experimental evasion in the two countries. The cross-national approach was more rewarding in the next series of experiments.

4 Framing, opportunity, and individual differences

4.1 Theoretical background

Weigel, Hessing, and Elffers' (1987) model treats evasion as a social dilemma and focuses on situational instigations (e.g. social norms) and constraints (e.g. opportunity) and psychological instigations (personal orientation) and constraints (perceived lack of opportunity, perceived risk). In this chapter, the effects of two independent variables are explored, namely decision frames and opportunity to evade. The experiments reported in this chapter provide evidence bearing on our model and Kahneman and Tversky's prospect theory (see 1.2). Support for the model will be evident also from the correlational patterns that have been found in the individual studies between fiscal behaviour and selected variables. The chapter divides neatly into three sections. In the first we discuss the background to the research, paying particular attention to the problem of framing. In the second we describe two of our early attempts to operationalise the 'opportunity' variable. These use a form of the landscape-gardener simulation. In the third we describe our most recent simulation, which is considerably more complex than the earlier versions and which allows for both income and deduction fraud. Here four studies are described which all have the same basic design (both framing and opportunity are manipulated) and which are part of a wider international project into tax evasion which is reported in Robben *et al.* (1990).

4.1.1 Framing

Unlike most models of tax compliance, we do not necessarily assume that (income) taxes are continuously salient to taxpayers. Nor do we believe that taxpayers are continually deliberating whether or not to comply, and if they decide not to, that they are constantly assessing the amounts and avenues used to fulfil that goal. An exception needs to be made for those taxpayers with sufficient knowledge and funds and for whom it is worthwhile to expend much money and effort in these activities. We do assume, however, that when taxpayers are thinking about their taxes, during the tax season in general and when completing their tax return in particular, they process the information available to them in such a manner that positive and negative

79

outcomes are weighted and considered in the light of their instigations and constraints (Kinsey 1988; Weigel, Hessing & Elffers 1987). By information available we mean, in addition to official tax guides, information that is presented to them by friends, newspapers and information that was already stored in long-term memory.

In describing taxpayer decision making, Carroll (1987, 1989) notes that a condition of relative inertia is characteristic of most taxpayers. Inertia may result in noncompliance when taxpayers do not file a return. It may also be viewed as a state of passivity, where situational changes are ignored. Then we are talking about habitual action. The question that comes to mind is: what are the conditions that cause an individual to break through the inertia or to change his or her behaviour? This directs our attention to those social situations that yield more reflective and deliberate decision making, for instance, by increasing the saliency of taxes (Kinsey 1988).

Saliency of taxes may be increased at the beginning of the tax season, when numerous governmental or commercial publications try to get our attention for one or another fiscal issue. It is equally possible for salience to increase at the end of the calendar year, when, at least in the Netherlands, attention is focused on the possibilities that are still open to pay some extra bills in order to pass a certain threshold for deductions, or to buy this year's individual retirement account (this is a tax deductible account which provides a benefit on retirement). Fiscal issues may also be made more salient by debates on tax reform, which have taken place in many countries recently, where all kinds of fiscal details are widely publicised, in quality journals as well as local papers, thus targeting a very large audience.

The point is that most people are probably unaware of fiscal matters for most of the time. They probably do not spend much time throughout the year thinking about possible avenues of 'saving' taxes. Setting aside the determined tax planner, we feel that income taxes are not on everybody's mind, let alone that people are constantly on the outlook for better and more rewarding evasion possibilities. Of course, part of this 'inertia' may be caused by the effects of previous tax planning, a result of which may be that the individual need not worry about these matters as they already have been arranged. This state of inertia may be broken through by information provided by others, e.g. tax consultants and colleagues.

Once an individual has come to the point at which fiscal decisions of the sort we are interested in here are taken, the question becomes how is that decision shaped? What are the influential variables? As we have explained earlier, we believe that fiscal behaviour in general, and tax evasion in particular, is determined by the interaction between an individual and his environment. However, we are inclined to emphasise individual factors in the decision-making process. Therefore a more or less cognitive approach is presented here to deal with that part of the process where the individual judges the tax situation and tries to respond appropriately to it.

In recent years, behavioural decision theory has attracted the attention of many tax researchers. In this approach, people are seen as active decision makers. Decisions pertain to various actions, accumulating in taxpaying behaviour, with each action having many alternatives. We make decisions about our earnings (will we take that second job or do some overtime?), about our investments (is an offshore account appropriate?), and about our outgoings, as well as collecting and organising tax records, and deciding how to file our return. The approach then considers the rationality of people in making their decisions (e.g. Becker 1968). Several authors in the tax-compliance field have argued that taxpayers are only partially rational (Scholz 1985; Carroll 1987). In contrast, economic models of tax evasion generally assume that people are amoral rational decision makers and treat evasion as a simple gamble (Allingham & Sandmo 1972).

The bounded rationality view is fairly typical for complex behaviours that require much of the individual's financial and behavioural resources. Given this limited cognitive ability, how do people (in this case taxpayers) cope with the complexity of the situation? Several strategies are at hand, such as decomposing complex problems into components that may be solvable or the development of habits or standardised routines which change only when they appear to be inadequate, for instance when a more profitable or less stressful solution becomes available (March & Simon 1958; Cyert & March 1963). As tax laws are omnipresent and applicable to large sections of our societies, we think about taxes regularly and in varying depth. So the notion of developing a routine behaviour to cope with official tax requirements is quite appealing (Kinsey 1988), although we sense a slight disagreement about the extent to which taxpayers' behaviour really is routinised (Scholz 1985; Carroll 1987).

Breaking down a decision regarding taxpaying behaviour can be accomplished in several ways. Weaver and Carroll (1985) distinguish between the decision to act like a criminal or to stop such behaviour (a 'career' or strategic decision), and a decision to be on the lookout for certain opportunities (a 'job' or tactical decision). As there are obviously many avenues for coming to a decision, Carroll (1987) argues that a certain strategy should be chosen. Although this may seem to lead to possible regressions *ad infinitum* (a strategy needed to choose a strategy to choose a strategy), this hierarchy of strategies can be applied to taxpayers' behaviour. The taxpayer who copies a friend's tax return is said to use a relatively low-level strategy, whereas the taxpayer incorporating his friends' strategies by using their returns as guidelines where they resemble his situation, and using other information in places where they provide no guidelines, clearly acts according to a higher-level strategy.

Before entering the decision process, then, the taxpayer is required to separate the situation into parts as alternatives, outcomes and reference points (Kahneman & Tversky 1979). However, Baldry (1986) has shown that decision problems that are formally equivalent may evoke quite different behaviour if they are perceived differently. In this study, identical experiments 'dressed up' as either tax or gambling situations gave quite different results. By editing or framing the situation, a simplification occurs that directs the attention to specific constituents of the restructured problem. Depending on how the taxpayer frames his situation, different behaviours may occur, as strategies now may be employed to comply with tax laws or defy them (Scholz 1985). This concern with how situations are perceived ties in with the work of Kahneman and Tversky (1979, 1984). In their prospect theory they have argued that people make choices in two stages. In the first stage, the problem-editing phase, the individual reformulates options so that the subsequent choice is simplified. An important part of this process is the framing of outcomes (prospects) as gains or losses, relative to some reference point. In the second stage, the evaluation phase, the individual evaluates each of the edited prospects and chooses the prospect with the highest value. In this stage the individual will use a utility function which is convex for losses, concave for gains and steeper for losses than for gains. This implies that when sure gains are involved individuals will tend to avoid risks, whereas they will be willing to take risks to avoid sure losses. It also implies that people will take different decisions depending on how problems are framed. The relevance of behavioural decision theory to tax evasion has been noted by a number of researchers (e.g. Carroll 1987; Loftus 1985; Smith & Kinsey 1987; Weigel, Hessing & Elffers 1987; Casey & Scholz, in press).

Following this theoretical analysis one might wonder whether any empirical basis exists that justifies the application of prospect theory to the tax domain. We will examine this scarce information briefly, both on an individual (perception) basis and on an aggregate level.

We will give one example from the experimental domain. Using hypothetical tax-declaration situations, Chang, Nichols, and Schulz (1987) instructed a sample of executive MBA students to perform a rating task. The descriptions of the hypothetical situations included the operationalisations of three independent variables: the amount of savings when not reporting the income from a second source, audit probabilities, and the extent of the financial penalties if caught. Subjects had to indicate whether or not they would report a certain amount derived from an extra income source. This task was followed by a questionnaire which among other things required the subjects to indicate whether they perceived the tax payments on the additional income to be a reduced gain or a pure loss.

The results provide evidence for the prospect theoretical notions. In the group of participants who perceived their situation as a reduced gain, 23% indicated they would cheat under the conditions provided. This percentage rose to 65% for those who reported a negative pay-off situation. Two other studies show mixed results, most probably because the intended decision frames were not induced in the subjects (Hite, Jackson & Spicer 1988; Schadewald 1989).

On an aggregate level there are the analyses done by Cox and Plumley (1988) on the voluntary compliance rates for a sample of 50,000 1982 tax returns. Their analyses indicate that income-tax compliance varies as a function of the size of taxpayers' refund or balance due. The results of these analyses are summarised in Figure 4.1.

Cox and Plumley employ the 'voluntary compliance rate', which for a given tax return represents the percentage of the total tax liability actually paid with tax liability determined by government audit of the return. It thus depicts the relative proportion of taxes owed that have already been paid by the taxpayer without any outside pressure from the revenue services. The analyses start by separating income sources from wages or salaries and business income, and dividing taxpayers into those who expected to get a refund from those who anticipated an additional payment. These comparisons are graphically illustrated in Figure 4.1.

Figure 4.1 compares the voluntary compliance rates of taxpayers who received a refund with taxpayers whose withholding taxes were insufficient to cover their tax debt and, hence, had a balance due. For taxpayers whose primary income source was wages or salaries (indicated by the line combining solid dots), the overall voluntary compliance rate was 95%. However, the voluntary compliance rate was higher (96%) for individuals whose returns claimed a refund of more than $1,000 and lower (89%) for taxpayers facing a 'balance due' of over $1,000. For business income (indicated by the line combining the circles), the results were even more dramatic. Here the voluntary compliance rate was 95% for individuals anticipating a refund in excess of $1,000 versus 70% for taxpayers who owed a balance of more than $1,000. As can be inferred from the downwardly sloping curves for both types of income sources, the voluntary compliance rate diminished as refunds became smaller and further diminished as the size of the 'balance due' increased. Whether the relatively linear patterns which emerged in Figure 4.1 would be sustained if other potentially confounded variables (e.g. age, sex, perceived risk of punishment, attitudes towards tax cheating, level of income and tax situation, use of paid preparers) were controlled, cannot be determined from these data.

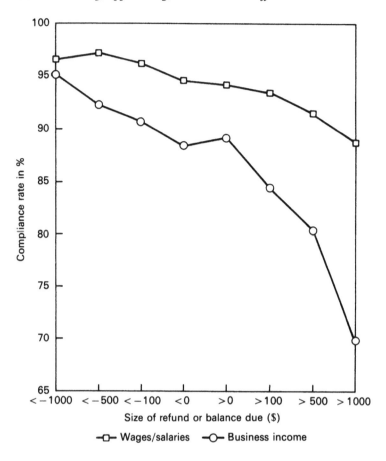

Figure 4.1   Voluntary compliance rate as a function of the size of refund or balance due.

As we have asserted above, we (and many others) view prospect theory as an extremely promising tool to investigate the effects of different tax-withholding effects, an important variable in our social psychological model of tax-evasion behaviour. Several of the experiments reported below were designed to test hypotheses regarding the process of the tax-evasion decision. This is not to signify that we assert that we measured the process in the laboratory, but more or less than we tried to influence it using our experimental manipulations. Although we share Carroll's view that the process of making decisions itself represents a variable, in that 'taxpayers may switch back and forth between self-aware and deliberate decision-making and habitual, unthoughtful carrying out of procedures' (1987, 328), no attempts have been undertaken to investigate this in our research to date.

4.1.2 *Opportunity*

Taxpayers vary in terms of the opportunities available to them to conceal income or declare unwarranted deductions. Greater opportunity is generally associated with self-employment and income sources not subject to withholding taxes. With one exception (Mason & Calvin 1978), surveys have consistently shown that respondents who are self-employed are more likely to admit various forms of noncompliance with tax laws (Aitkin & Bonneville 1980; Groenland & Van Veldhoven 1983; Mason & Lowry 1981). Similarly, 39% of Vogel's Swedish respondents (Vogel 1974) who acknowledged receiving additional income that was not taxable at the source also admitted evading taxes as compared to 21% of those acknowledging no such additional income. In addition, Wärneryd and Walerud (1982) found significant correlations between self-reported opportunity and admitted evasion. Opportunity has been reported as the most important explanatory factor in several investigations (Clotfelter 1983; Slemrod 1985; Witte & Woodbury 1985; Laurin 1986). De Juan (1989) found in her questionnaire study that self-reported opportunity to evade taxes was correlated with being a male, self-employed, being satisfied with the personal economical situation, risk-prone, knowing others who have evaded tax, moonlighting, and having political resources.

The survey findings are supported by other evidence suggesting the impact of opportunity on tax-evasion behaviour. For example, 43% of Wallschutzky's (1984) sample of convicted evaders were self-employed as opposed to 13% of the nonevaders. In addition, the recent Internal Revenue Service analyses reported in Figure 1.1 also shed some light on the link between opportunity and noncompliance. Disregarding the taxpayers' refund or balance due status, these data indicate that the percentage of the total tax liability voluntarily reported was considerably higher for wage earners (95%) than for individuals whose primary source of income was business related (77%). Also, Long and Swingen (1988) have shown using a structural equation model that opportunity, as indexed by third-party reporting has a strong impact on noncompliance. Using 1982 and 1985 TCMP data, Long and Swingen (1989) compared misreporting rates for line items before and after the introduction of new third-party reporting requirements which reduced the opportunity for evasion. They report significant reductions in both under- and overreporting tax errors after the introduction of these reports. The overall consistency of these findings, despite substantial variation in the procedures used to measure opportunity, suggests the importance of the opportunity dimensions for increasing or inhibiting tax-evasion behaviour.

None the less the causal position of opportunity is unclear. It could be that individuals who are predisposed to evade taxes seek and obtain jobs where there are many opportunities for evasion, whereas those who are compliant by inclination do not. This would make opportunity just an indicator of relevant individual differences. Experimentation is useful to establish whether opportunity does have a genuine causal role.

4.2   Two studies into the opportunity to evade

The next two studies were the first investigations to address the role of opportunity in an experimental setting. Both were carried out in the UK.

4.2.1   *UK08: Opportunity, audit probability, and values*

In this study we manipulated 'opportunity to evade' by giving participants two income streams, one official, one unofficial. In addition we tried to devise a more realistic manipulation of audit probability. A third focus was individual differences in values. There were two main reasons for believing that the values people hold may influence their evasion behaviour. First, on the basis of work carried out in related fields, Cialdini (1989) suggests several norms/values that may be associated with taxpayer compliance. He mentions concepts like social responsibility, personal integrity, paying one's way, and patriotism. Negative influences are represented by such values as cheating, stealing, lying, criminal action, harming others, and weakening the nation (Cialdini 1989, 209). Second, Kristiansen (1985) showed that value rankings predicted preventive health behaviour, a finding that raises questions about Fishbein and Ajzen's (1975) notion that specific attitudes are needed to predict specific behaviours and which suggests exploring the relevance of values to tax behaviour.

Method
Subjects   Forty-eight undergraduate students took part, recruited from and tested in a University Hall of Residence. There were 21 males and 27 females.
Design   This was based on that used for UK05 ('landscape gardener'), though a number of modifications were made to the program. Changes were made to manipulate opportunity and audit probability and to further enhance the experimental realism of the task.

The principal task-related change was to alter the time structure of the simulation. In the original version, the simulation was divided into two years and each year divided into six two-month periods. Participants had to make four decisions (including making a tax return) each period. It was felt that this overemphasised the tax aspect of the situation, since no one makes income-tax declarations every two months. In the version used in this study, the simulation was divided into twelve six-month periods (April–September and October–March) and tax returns made annually. To emphasise the division of each year into summer and winter, at the beginning of each period a teletext news page dated appropriately was displayed on the screen for thirty seconds. The teletext displays were near-perfect imitations of those used on Independent Television's ORACLE service. They differed from the real thing only in being one column width narrower. They covered a variety of topics, some being actual 'human interest' stories taken from the daily papers ('Mr Jack Mouncey, a senior manager, was dominated while at home by his wife who sometimes made him sleep in the car'), others being fabricated ('An exhibition entitled "Degas to Dali" opened today at the Royal Academy, London').

To make the task more involving, the demand for landscape services altered in the winter. Making demand a function of price, amount of advertising *and* season made achieving the optimum price more of a challenge. In addition those features specifically relating to management were deleted, i.e. the initial screen display and the opening sentence of the instructions, and the cost of information and advertising made more realistic (information £150 per bit, advertising £240 per unit).

Opportunity was manipulated by providing subjects with an unofficial source of income. For the half in the high opportunity condition, each summer, after they had set their charges, they saw this screen display: 'You have agreed to do some weekend work. It will last about x weekends. What price are you going to charge per hour for this?' The value of x was preset and varied between 2 and 5. After they had entered their weekend charge there was a pause and then a display announced what their weekend receipts were. Their receipts from their main job were adjusted appropriately so that those in the high-opportunity condition did not earn more overall than those in the low-opportunity condition.

The audit probability variable was manipulated by presenting half of the subjects with a different teletext news story in the winter of the second year. Half the subjects saw a story headlined 'INLAND REVENUE WORK TO RULE', which continued, 'Union officials today confirmed their intention to work to rule at the Inland Revenue in pursuit of a 9.5% pay rise. A Home Office spokesman commented that this action was most likely to hurt senior citizens and the recently unemployed, who would not receive tax rebates. However, the union pointed out that in order to hit government revenue they would not be issuing new tax codings nor auditing businesses.' The other half read an innocuous story headlined 'Princess Alexandra attends film première.'

No information was given about audit frequency or fine rates. This minimises the obtrusiveness of the tax aspect of the study and makes the situation more comparable to the everyday context. In fact, everybody was audited once. This was predetermined such that equal numbers of subjects were audited in each of the six years. If an individual did evade in the year a £500 fine was imposed.

Procedure   The first part of the study consisted of the simulation, which on average took about forty minutes. Subjects subsequently completed a modified Rokeach (1973) value survey, which was implemented on the microcomputer to make it easy for them to do the ranking task. The instructions for this were as follows:

> In this study you are asked to rank 9 values. These will appear on the screen in alphabetical order. Your task is to arrange them in order of their importance to you, as guiding principles in your life. Study the list carefully and pick out the value which is the most important for you. Assign to this value the number 1. Then pick out the value which is second most important to you. Assign to this value the number 2. Then do the same for each of the remaining values, until you have included all ranks from 1 to 9. Each value should have a different rank. Make sure that there are no ties! Work slowly and think carefully. If you change your mind, feel free to change your answers.

> We realise that some people find it difficult to distinguish the importance of some of these values. The end result should truly show how you really feel. It is important for you to notice that there are no right or wrong ranks to the values. All we are interested in is your private ranking of the values.

The following nine values were presented: a sense of achievement, a world of beauty, equality, family security, honesty, inner harmony, mature love, national security, social recognition.

Results
The data were analysed using two $2 \times 2 \times 6$ analyses of variance with opportunity (2 levels), audit probability (2 levels), and year of audit (6 levels) as between-groups factors. There were no significant results for either the frequency of underdeclaring or the percentage of income not declared (see Table 4.1). Correlations between the value rankings and evasion were uniformly low. The highest (yet still nonsignificant) correlation was between social recognition and percentage of income declared ($r = 0.14$).

Discussion
These results are disappointing and provide no evidence that any of the factors under investigation are relevant. Why is this the case? We believe that the manipulation of audit probability was not salient enough and that manipulating opportunity is simply more difficult than it appears.

There were two problems with the audit probability manipulation. First, news stories other than the 'Inland Revenue' story were irrelevant to the

Table 4.1. *Mean number of times (out of 6) that income was underdeclared and mean percentage not declared (in brackets) as a function of audit probability and opportunity to evade (N = 48)*

		Audit probability		
		Low	High	Average
Opportunity	High	2.3 (12)	3.1 (4)	2.7 (9)
	Low	1.8 (9)	2.6 (24)	2.2 (16)
	Average	2.0 (10)	2.8 (14)	2.4 (12)

task. Second, there was nothing in the instructions given at the beginning to highlight the importance of the teletext stories. Thus the stories are trivialised and subjects had no reason to pay any attention to them (other than for light relief). It is easy to overcome these difficulties and the subsequent study does so.

That the manipulation of opportunity failed is more of a problem. It is possible that providing subjects with some income which is ideally suited to nondeclaration makes the decision to evade easier but also encourages the evasion of small amounts since the unofficial income is only a small fraction of total earnings. The figures in Table 4.1 are suggestive. Those with unofficial earnings evaded more often overall (2.7 compared to 2.2) but evaded less of their income (9.4% compared to 16.3%).

The uninteresting correlations of evasion with the value rankings could be due to shortcomings of the method. A very limited set of values was used (Rokeach 1973 described eighteen terminal values of which we used eight plus one of the 'instrumental values') and this may have made the measurement too coarse. But it is more likely that these values do not influence evasion. Montgomery, Drottz, Gärling, Persson, and Waara (1985) have pointed out that Rokeach's taxonomy of values is inadequate and that many important ones are excluded. More importantly, some of those that are included (such as 'honest' and 'social recognition') were hardly ever mentioned by respondents in Montgomery *et al.*'s survey. This suggests that they are not core guiding principles. There is another factor that is relevant. Henry (1978) and others have shown that people make a sharp distinction between behaviour towards others and behaviour towards institutions. Thus even if 'honesty' is important to an individual, it may well not influence his or her evasion behaviour, as it probably will be regarded as an action towards the state, the largest institution most individuals are faced with.

4.2.2   UK09: Opportunity, audit probability, alienation, and attitudes towards the law

This study was intended to be an improved version of the previous one, with the same factors being manipulated (opportunity to evade and audit probability). As measuring values had not proved useful we focused instead on individual differences in alienation and attitude towards the law, both of which had proved successful predictors in previous studies.

Method

Subjects   Fifty-two undergraduate students taking psychology as an ancillary subject took part. They were tested in three batches.

Design   This was based on that used for UK08 though a number of modifications were made to the program to make the manipulation of audit probability more salient. In addition the simulation lasted five rather than six years. As before, opportunity was manipulated by providing subjects with an unofficial source of income.

To make the teletext pages more salient a sentence was added to the 'Information' section of the instructions ('In addition, you will receive a free teletext service (a news page) which may sometimes contain helpful information') and new teletext stories written which would be of relevance to a landscape-gardening firm. Thus the first story focused on a rise in the rate of inflation and the second on the news that Exeter would be staging the next International Garden Festival. This included the information that 'Councillor Mark McNair, who will be chairing the organising committee, said that the Festival should boost tourism and the demand for gardening services in the South-West.' Later stories included one headlined 'QUEEN MUM OPENS FLOWER SHOW.' The audit probability variable was manipulated, as before, with the 'INLAND REVENUE WORK TO RULE' story.

Procedure   The first part of the study consisted of the simulation, which on average took about thirty-five minutes. Forty of the subjects subsequently completed the first part of the questionnaire used in UK07, which measured alienation and attitude to the law.

Results

The data were analysed using two 2×2 analyses of variance with opportunity (2 levels) and audit probability (2 levels) as factors. For both the frequency of underdeclaring and the percentage of income declared there was a significant effect of audit probability ($F = 4.7$, $df = 1,48$, $p < 0.05$; $F = 5.1$, $df = 1,48$, $p < 0.05$). There were no other significant effects (see Table 4.2). Only scores on the attitude to the law scale were significantly related to evasion (see Table 4.3).

Table 4.2. *Mean number of times (out of 5) that income was underdeclared and mean percentage of income not declared (in brackets) as a function of audit probability and opportunity to evade (N=40)*

		Audit probability		
		Low	High	Average
Opportunity	High	2.2 (11)	1.5 (8)	1.8 (9)
	Low	3.6 (27)	2.0 (6)	2.8 (16)
	Average	2.9 (19)	1.7 (6)	2.3 (13)

Table 4.3. *Correlations between tax evasion and attitude measures (N=40)*

	Number of periods in which tax was evaded	Percentage of income undeclared
Attitude towards law	-0.33^{**}	-0.28^{*}
Alienation	-0.05	0.12

Note: one-tailed probabilities are $^{**}p<0.025$, $^{*}p<0.05$.
A high score on the attitude towards law indicates a more positive stance towards law in general; a high score on the alienation measure indicates more alienation from society.

Discussion

Altering the salience of the teletext pages clearly had the intended effect; when tax inspectors were on strike, the frequency of evasion increased and the percentage of income declared dropped. Surprisingly, those given an unofficial source of income declared more income. This is not significant but is puzzling none the less. Our interpretation is that we had unwittingly manipulated feelings of success. Being asked to carry out weekend work suggests that your services are in great demand and that you are running your business well. This feeling of success may well lead to less evasion, perhaps mediated by the belief that you are doing better than others (see the results of UK05).

That attitude towards the law is related to evasion in the simulation is encouraging and replicates our earlier findings. However, alienation, which has been a good predictor in the past, here is not. We have no explanation for this.

4.3   Introduction to the improved simulations

The task in the next simulations differed considerably from that used in all the previous experiments. Given our criticism of the quality of the dependent variable in earlier studies our use of simple declarations is hard to justify. So here tax declarations resembled real-life returns more closely than ever, as both a declaration of the earned income and of allowable deductions were required from the subjects. This feature was introduced by asserting that '. . . undoubtedly, you will incur all kinds of expenses while running your business. In this simulation, you will be allowed to deduct all the expenses from your gross business result.'

The amount of taxes withheld was introduced as the second manipulation. As mentioned in section 4.1.1, several investigations have tried to show a relationship between the amount in taxes due for refund or additional payment and noncompliance. The amount is used as a proxy for the self-reported financial strain the situation imposes on the individual. The strain variable has been incorporated into several models of tax evasion (Wärneryd & Walerud 1982; Weigel, Hessing & Elffers 1987).

Associated with the amount to be settled with the revenue service is the individual's appreciation of the situation. Although a certain payment may be proportionally low or high to one's income, relative to a certain anchoring point the result may be judged positively or negatively. As has been mentioned in the introduction section of this chapter, prospect theory seems a promising avenue along which to investigate this concept of subjective strain acting as an individual instigation to tax evasion.

4.3.1   *Overview of instructions*

To present an overall picture of the information we confronted our subjects with, we would like to give a summary of the instructions used in the next four studies. These instructions generally were updated when necessary or changed where appropriate to support local conditions. The text in this section is a translation of that actually used in NL02 and NL03. The sections described below are presented in the same order as they appeared on the screen for the participants. In some experiments, we had a training period before the real simulation began. During that training, all decisions that would be made in the real run were practised. Decisions on buying information, advertising, improving the business, pricing, and copying down financial information had to be made in each of the periods. Tax returns were completed annually.

Introductory section   The first screens were designed to familiarise the participants with the different parts of the computer, especially the keyboard. Throughout the simulation a limited number of keys were used to guide the subjects through the investigation. The placement and the meaning of these keys were explained in some detail. Furthermore, we made clear that 'We would like you to go through the investigation on your own. This means without the help of other participants, or without helping them.' We also tried to reassure people that there would be no problem should they make a mistake, e.g. when entering a number, as sufficient opportunity would be provided to correct any figure they typed in.

We then moved on to say something on the rationale for the study, which read: 'This investigation has been developed for researching economic behaviour in small enterprises. You have to imagine that you set yourself up as a shopkeeper running a small supermarket.' After explaining that their task would last for two years with each of both years consisting of two periods, subjects were informed that in each period, they 'will have to make a number of financial decisions, just like a shopkeeper in the real world has to face'.

Going into more detail, the text read:

> Part of your considerations will be the decision whether or not to advertise your firm and products. Also, whether or not you are willing to spend money on improving your business services has to be determined. To base your decisions on more solid grounds, you can buy additional information. This information has been collected by a local advertising agency. For the above purposes you will be offered a set of alternatives regarding advertising and investment possibilities, as well as different sets of information to choose from. And, of course, you will have to decide upon the selling prices of your products. At the end of each year you will have to make a tax return, and to pay taxes on the amount declared.
>
> Your task will be to run your shop as successfully as possible.

Now we tried to explain the pricing decisions, by alluding to the fact they needed to price their products sensibly, as both over- and underdemand would have negative consequences. For practical reasons, we honestly said, the pricing task was necessarily limited to only two products in each period, with preset price ranges to help subjects determine the 'correct' prices. Setting prices, buying additional information, advertising the firm and the products, and spending money on improving the business's service were all mentioned as constituting parts of a general strategy they could work out.

Fiscal information was provided as well. This read:

> The tax rate in the investigation will be 33%. Taxes will be withheld in advance on the basis of an estimated yearly business result. The tax inspector uses your first results for this estimation. At the end of each year, when you file your tax return, it will become evident whether the amount estimated by the tax inspector was correct, or either too low or

too high. This will result in either an additional payment from your side
or in a tax refund by the tax inspector. Tax returns are checked on a
random basis, and you will be informed about whether your return has
been audited.

The tax rate used in the study is in fact a compromise rate, but it is plausible
for both countries. Participants were told their financial situation would be
presented on the screen after each period, which they needed to copy down
on worksheets provided. This procedure then would facilitate their completion of each year's tax return.

After these introductory screens, the necessary actions were summarised
on a separate screen, and sometimes provided in writing as well.

Information provided   As mentioned above, at the beginning of each period
subjects could buy additional information regarding their business decisions
if they wanted to. They could choose information on four topics: Trends in the
market, Pricing in the retail business, Seasonal effects on sales, and On the
usefulness of advertising. While the contents of these topics did not change
between the years, we decided to change it per period, where possible, to
make the task more involving by relating the information to the time of year.

So in the first period, 'Trends in your market' would read:

> Research in economics has shown how difficult it is to accurately predict
> the state of the market and movements therein. The latter half of last
> year has been rather successful for most retailers. People reported on
> average a higher turnover and higher profits than in previous years.
>
> In the opinion of leading experts in the field a small economic set-back is
> likely to occur in the present period. Although they see no reason to
> worry, turnovers probably will decrease. As a result, profits will decline as
> well.

– thus suggesting a bit of pessimism (we adjusted the taxable incomes
accordingly). Period 2, however, predicted a sunnier view:

> Although accurate predictions on how the economy and the market for
> your products will develop are difficult to make, there is some consensus
> on what may be expected in the near future. Experts feel that there is a
> tendency for turnovers, and thus profits as well, to increase in the second
> part of this year.
>
> This statement is supported by recent research which shows that many
> consumers expect a small improvement in the economy. It is assumed
> that people will have more money to spend, and that this will make
> consumers buy more.

Advertising possibilities   We tried to provide a selection of opportunities that
would contain both sufficient realism and excitement to make it an involving
task for the subject. So in each year they could choose between three
possibilities (remaining equal in the periods). For year 1 these were the local

paper, the radio, or the local cinema. In year 2, the advertising media were altered into sponsoring a sports club, financing a trip of the local choir to a festival, and having a message on electronic display in the local buses.

If a participant opted for the last alternative, a set of screens like those below would appear on the computer monitor:

THE ELECTRONIC NEWSPAPER
Advertising on an electronic newspaper on local coach lines is a new way to spread your name and promote your firm. How does this work?

In front of the coach a screen is fixed on which messages are displayed throughout the journey. As most passengers will be facing the front of the coach, chances are great that many will actually read your message.

A big advantage is that you can change your advertisement immediately, which allows you to react to movements in your market almost instantaneously. You can choose the time at which your message should be displayed daily.

The degree to which coaches are occupied varies over the day, and during peak hours you expect to reach far more people than during other hours. However, this is of course more expensive.

Listed below are the times at which your messages may be displayed on the electronic newspaper, and the corresponding costs.

0. I changed my mind; I shall not advertise.
1. Between 07.00 and 09.30 hours; costs . . .
2. Between 09.30 and 13.00 hours; costs . . .
3. Between 13.00 and 16.00 hours; costs . . .
4. Between 16.00 and 17.30 hours; costs . . .
5. Between 17.30 and 21.00 hours; costs . . .

Please state the interval of your preference.

Having stated a preferred interval, the following message appeared, 'You have bought . . . worth of advertising', and the subject moved on to the next decision: investments by improving his or her business service.
Improving service   We introduced this by telling participants that

By investing carefully and on time you may maintain or even increase your sales. For example, you may hire an assistant for the ever so busy weekends. Also, you can contract a designer to have the shop's interior re-modelled, or buy a new van to improve your delivery-at-home service.

Experience has shown that these kinds of investments are earned back within one and a half years. Do you want to invest money in this period y(es)/n(o)?

An affirmative reply would lead to a screen providing the subject with some more information:

What amount do you wish to spend this period on the improvement of your choice? You have to take into account that for all spendings there are minimum as well as maximum amounts. If you propose to do an investment which is less than the minimum rate then you can consider your order turned down.

However, if your proposed investment exceeds the going maximum rate it is rather unlikely that it will be profitable within a reasonable span of time. Chances are that indeed it may lead to a loss! The computer will warn you if your offer is outside one of the boundaries. If so, you will be given another opportunity to think of a more acceptable fee.

You may now indicate the investment of your preference.

    0. I do not want to improve my service now.
    1. I want to have a weekend shop assistant.
    2. I want to have the interior of the shop remodelled.
    3. I want to have a van for delivering orders.

Please choose by pressing 0, 1, 2 or 3.

Let us suppose that alternative 1 had been chosen. The following screens then appeared:

Hiring a shop assistant takes your mind off all kinds of tiresome activities. By letting someone else take care of many routine duties, you can spend your time at more important things.

Shop assistants come in many varieties, and very important, with different experience. A young assistant with hardly any experience will be happy with a relatively modest salary. An older and more experienced assistant may do the job better but will be more expensive as well.

To give you a guideline, here are the limits set to the assistant's salary:

Lowest amount . . .
Highest amount . . .

Entering and acknowledging an acceptable amount would display the message 'Your investments in this period amount to . . .'

Pricing decision   Finally, products needed to be priced. As stated earlier, only two types of products were chosen each period, although these differed from one period to the next. In this set of experiments, we decided to go for coffee, butter, electric bulbs, ball points, wholewheat cereal, baked beans, writing pads, cup and saucer, washing-powder, shampoo, frozen chicken, salad dressing, and soft drinks. The pricing decision was implemented like this:

Your shop is called Henry's Super. You can now set your selling prices for each product-line for this first part of year 1. Please type in your prices like this, for instance 1.95 or 2.50. After you have typed in your price, press key ⏎.

Product: ball points
Average cost price: £1.00
Your selling price: £

Product: writing pads
Average cost price: £1.75
Your selling price: £

Of course, prices could be changed to the subjects' wishes, and upon entering and acknowledging both prices, they were told, 'Your business result will be calculated according to these prices.'

The pricing decision was the last of the decisions we implemented to make the task interesting and involving for the subjects. These decisions and associated text screens were not included just for the fun of it. One of our aims in these simulations was to play down the tax aspect of the research as much as possible, and simultaneously to make the task less repetitive.

Semi-annual information The pricing decision brought the participants to the following financial overview for that period (the low opportunity condition in some of the experiments contained a random subset of three from the six deductible tax items below). The example was derived from a subject in the high opportunity and overwithholding condition (hence the six deductions and the higher amount of taxes actually paid):

Semi-annual report for year 1, part 1
INCOME [IN GUILDERS]

GROSS business result	52,400

EXPENSES – tax deductible.

Information	1,500
Advertising	2,000
Improvements	4,000
Rent	3,000
Energy	3,300
Administration	1,400
Your taxable income is	37,200
You have actually paid in taxes	17,233
33% of your taxable income is	12,276

PLEASE MAKE A COPY OF THIS SEMI-ANNUAL SUMMARY ON PAPER

Filing a tax return After two periods, a full year in business had come to an end, and thus a tax return was to be filed. Again, subjects were introduced to this part of the task by a new screen:

HOW TO MAKE YOUR TAX RETURN

You may now complete your tax return for year . . .. With the information you have copied at the end of each period this should be

relatively easy for you. First of all you complete the form marked TAX
RETURN for year . . . When finished, you type the amounts you want to
declare in the computer. The computer will assist you in this task. Just
type the amounts at the appropriate places, and the computer will do the
rest.

Some of the costs you have incurred can be deducted from your gross
income. In this investigation your taxable income is defined as your
income minus the expenses you have been allowed to deduct. After you
typed in a certain amount, press the ↵ key. When you have typed in all
amounts, just answer the questions that appear on the screen. You will
be allowed to make changes if you want to. Please act as you think fit.

Two additional screens appeared, allowing subjects to enter their figures
for both income declarations and the declaration of their tax-deductible
items. In both screens sufficient opportunity was provided for subjects to alter
the amounts they entered.

The first screen looked like this:

TAX RETURN FOR YEAR . . .

A.   INCOME [in guilders]

A1.	GROSS business results first part	52,400
A2.	GROSS business results second part	77,400
AT.	Total business result (calculated)	129,800 [guilders]

The second was as follows (the low opportunity condition in some of the
experiments contained a random subset of three from the six deductible tax
items below):

B.   EXPENSES – tax deductible [in guilders]

B1.	Information	3,000
B2.	Advertising	5,000
B3.	Improvements	6,000
B4.	Rent	6,000
B5.	Energy	6,600
B6.	Administration	2,400
BT.	Total costs deductible (calculated)	29,000

Having completed this, they were informed that 'You have now made all
necessary declarations for your tax return to be processed. At this moment
you can either file the tax return as it is, or you may alter it if necessary.'
Pressing F to file or R to review the return invoked the desired action,
eventually followed after a short delay (caused by the 'tax inspector'
processing the return) by a message saying, 'Your tax return has been filed
and been processed. No audit has been requested.'

Feedback on performance   Sending off the tax return for processing in all cases led to the message that no audit had been requested. In most experiments, a screen informing the participant of his financial status was presented, providing information on taxable income, taxes paid, fines paid, and net income for that year. At the end of the simulation, an overview was given. After the presentation of the results of each year, a message intended to stimulate the participants was projected on the screen, saying either 'Judging from the decisions you made during the last year, and looking at the income you earned, you have overall done a good job', or 'The way you acted throughout the years that you have been in business showed that you have a good understanding of what running a small shop is about.'

Manipulations   In order to increase the salience of the manipulations, we decided to implement them immediately *before* and *after* the subject needed to complete the tax return. Typically, such screens would have a header like 'On your tax return', and then describe some particular circumstance the subject had to attend to. For instance, in the high-opportunity condition, it was explained that 'You are now to declare your income. The tax inspectorate may otherwise not trace how much money you have made during the last year, as most of your income typically is earned in cash.' For the overwithholding condition, a screen containing the following message was displayed: 'Your withholding taxes are more than enough to cover your actual tax due this year. It appears that you will receive a substantial refund.' These texts would never come as a real surprise, however, as in the introductory sections we had already mentioned the income source or the traceability of income and the tax inspector's estimates about the correct tax liability.

4.4   NLO2: Withholding, opportunity, and attitudes

Method

Subjects   Seventy-one undergraduate students, most taking economics as their main subject, were recruited as participants. For reasons explained below, the final subject pool consisted of fifteen females and fifty-three males. In all, it took about forty minutes to complete the simulation. In addition, completing a postexperimental questionnaire featuring a number of attitude and personality scales took a similar amount of time. All participants were paid 15 guilders (approximately £4).

Design   In the low-opportunity condition, subjects were presented with three itemised deductions (costs incurred for obtaining additional information, advertising costs, and money spent on improving the business' service). In the high-opportunity condition, six itemised deductions were allowed (costs for rent, energy consumption, and administration were added).

The withholding factor was manipulated straightforwardly in this experiment. By presenting all subjects with an identical taxable income (unknown to them) tax payments were arranged so that at the end of the year half the participants were faced with a refund due, and the other half with an additional tax payment. This took place independently of their decisions during the simulation up to that point. The amounts at stake were identical for both conditions, but differed across the 'years' in the simulation to prevent subjects from recognising the same amounts in each year. This allowed for a standardised environment in which the effects of the predictors could be tested. Fixing the taxable income did reduce the significance of participants' behaviour somewhat, as this influenced only the *gross* business income.

Procedure   Subjects were assigned an identification number at random. The computer programme then determined the experimental condition for the subject. The simulation consisted of two years of two periods each. In addition to the decisions with regard to information, advertising, and improvements, subjects were presented with a semi-annual financial summary, to be copied down on worksheets that were provided for that goal. The summary listed gross business income for that period, expenses made (including those for rent, energy, and administration if in the high opportunity condition), taxable income, taxes withheld, and the 'correct' tax liability – either lower or higher than the amount of tax withheld. Through this summary subjects learned about their tax status, whether they were due for a refund or for an additional payment.

This was repeated at the end of the second period, thus leaving the subject with all the necessary information to complete the tax return for that year. For completing the tax return the subjects were required to type the amounts they wanted to declare for both income parts and, on a different screen, for the three or six expenses. They were given the opportunity to review or change the return before 'sending it off' to the tax authorities. After a short delay a message appeared saying that the return had been processed and that *no* audit had been undertaken. After that message the subject was informed about the taxes paid and those owed, so a certain amount would either be received as a refund or have to be paid as an extra payment.

After the simulation, a postexperimental questionnaire containing sociodemographics, manipulation checks, and several personality and attitude measures was provided (see Table 4.11).

Results

Two quantitative measures were taken from subjects' behaviour: the frequency of tax fraud and the amount of tax evaded in guilders. It was decided to use 'money amount' as the early Dutch programmes had recorded only the total amounts evaded, which made calculations of percentages

Table 4.4. *Mean number of times (out of 4) that taxes were evaded and mean amount in guilders not reported (in brackets) as a function of opportunity and decision frame* $(N=68)$

	Decision frame		
	Received refund	Made payment	Overall
Low opportunity	0.25 (428)	0.31 (113)	0.28 (270)
High opportunity	0.59 (4,512)	0.76 (3,685)	0.68 (4,099)
Overall	0.44 (2,543)	0.55 (1,953)	0.48 (2,242)

awkward. The frequency measure was an index ranging from 0 to 4, with 0 indicating no evasion and the occurrence of income or deduction fraud in either year adding one to the index. Subjects could thus evade by underdeclaring income, overdeclaring business costs, or by using both alternatives. The number of deduction deviations was twice that of income deviations (19 versus 9 cases).

These data were analysed using two two-way analyses of variance, with decision frame and opportunity as factors, and the results of these analyses are given in Table 4.4. Three subjects' data were not used in the analyses: two correctly guessed the purpose of the experiment, and another subject was treated as an outlier. There were no significant effects for the amount of taxes evaded. Opportunity yielded a significant effect on the frequency of tax fraud $(F=4.0, p<0.05)$ and the amount not reported $(F=6.1, p<0.05)$.

The overall rate of dishonest reporting was 36%, so just over one in three subjects fiddled their taxes. An additional analysis was performed using participants' perceptions of their situation. For each of the two tax-declaration situations, they were asked which description best fitted the situation they were faced with. Respondents were classified as perceiving a refund, perceiving an additional payment, or as perceiving the situation neutrally. With this classification a one-way analysis of variance was performed with the frequency measure as criterion variable. This proved to be more successful in prospect theoretical terms; the subjects who indicated that they needed to make an extra payment evaded tax more frequently than those who recalled receiving a refund $(F=2.62, p<0.1$ for the first declaration and $F=3.65, p<0.05$ for the second one). Also, these subjects evaded to greater extent $(F=3.39, p<0.05$ for the first declaration and $F=3.30, p<0.05$ for the second one). Table 4.5 shows these results, indicating that perception of the withholding situation influences subsequent tax-evasion behaviour.

Table 4.5. *Mean number of times (out of 4) that taxes were evaded and mean amount in guilders not reported (in brackets) as a function of perceived decision frame*

Perceived decision frame after first declaration		
Refund	Neutral	Payment
0.29	0.27	0.71
(154)	(864)	(4,348)
N = 24	N = 11	N = 31
Perceived decision frame after second declaration		
Refund	Neutral	Payment
0.31	0.18	0.76
(325)	(927)	(4,460)
N = 26	N = 11	N = 29

Discussion

This experiment provides strong support for the proposition that greater opportunity leads to greater tax evasion and some support for prospect theory. That the effect of decision frame was comparatively small was probably due to the nature of the manipulation (the refund/payment was a very small part of a complicated business task), an interpretation supported by the fact that one-sixth of the participants did not know whether they had received a refund or a payment.

   None the less, our results must be treated with some caution. It is possible that students are not a good sample and that ideally members of the general public should be used. However, DeJong, Forsythe, and Uecker (1988) showed that businessmen subjects gave comparable data to student subjects in sealed-offer laboratory markets, which suggests that students may not be atypical. Further, although we have obtained evidence that opportunity is important, the exact nature of this variable is unclear. It may be, for instance, that people believe that a large number of fraudulent but small deductions are less likely to be detected than one large fraudulent deduction. Thus the crucial factor may be 'detectability' rather than opportunity.

4.5   NL03: Withholding, opportunity, and attitudes

This study is very similar to the one reported above. Some improvements were made to the opportunity variable, aimed at strengthening the effects of the manipulations.

Method

Subjects   Eighty-eight undergraduate students participated, 68 men and 20 women, most taking economics as their main subject. They responded to an advertisement in the university's newspaper announcing a research project investigating economic behaviour.

Design   Basically, the design is as above but various alterations were made to the manipulations of the opportunity variable. First, the operationalisation of 'low opportunity' was changed. A set of three tax-deductible items was randomly drawn for each individual subject from the set of six itemisable deductions arranged for the high-opportunity condition. This means that individual preferences for one or other deduction could no longer have a systematic effect on outcomes. Second, opportunity was strengthened by a message immediately before the tax-declaration screen. For the low-opportunity condition it read that most of the customers paid in cheques, which would be cleared through the company's bank account, thus leaving traces by which the tax authorities could easily investigate the real business income. In contrast, those in the high-opportunity condition were told their income derived mainly from cash receipts, which would be very difficult to verify by the revenue authorities should they wish to do so. For a rationale, one can think of the visibility of income as an opportunity for incorrectly completing tax forms (Kagan 1989, 81–2).

Procedure   Participants were tested in groups of varying size in several batches during a limited period in term time. The study was split into three parts. After the simulation, a computerised measurement of individual social orientation was administered (Liebrand's Decomposed Games 1984). Upon completion, a postexperimental questionnaire was provided, measuring socio-demographics, perception of the manipulations, and attitude and personality characteristics (see Table 4.11). All participants were paid 15 guilders (just over £4) upon delivery of the questionnaire.

Results

Identical quantitative measures as in NLO2 were used. Again, deduction fraud was more prevalent than income fraud (37 versus 26 cases). The withholding manipulation proved successful as significant effects were found for the frequency of evasion ($F = 4.6$, $p < 0.05$) and the effect approached significance for the amount evaded in guilders ($F = 3.7$, $p < 0.06$) (see Table 4.6). For amount, there was a significant effect in the expected direction for the opportunity variable ($F = 4.7$, $p < 0.05$).

The postexperimental questionnaire allowed us to check how subjects perceived their financial situation after the declaration. A slightly different measure than in NLO2 was used, which looked at *how* they perceived their

Table 4.6. *Mean number of times (out of 4) that taxes were evaded and amount in guilders not reported (in brackets) as a function of opportunity and decision frame (N=88)*

	Decision frame		
	Received refund	Made payment	Overall
Low opportunity	0.59 (2,894)	1.06 (4,026)	0.82 (3,460)
High opportunity	0.44 (4,416)	1.33 (13,493)	0.91 (9,222)
Overall	0.52 (3,632)	1.20 (8,895)	0.87 (6,341)

Table 4.7. *Mean number of times (out of 4) that taxes were evaded and amount in guilders not reported (in brackets) as a function of perceived decision frame*

Perceived decision frame	
Gain	Loss
0.40	1.16
(2,660)	(10,062)
N=25	N=19

refund or payment. Those participants indicating that they viewed their payment as a loss, evaded taxes significantly more frequently than those who perceived a neutral situation, or who saw their position as a gain (see Table 4.7; $t = -2.0$, $df=43$, $p<0.05$).

Discussion

Contrary to our NLO2 study, the decision-frame variable showed the expected effects on both dependent measures. This is surprising as the manipulations used were the same in both experiments; nevertheless, we have some ideas on what may have caused this divergence. Several differences between NLO2 and NLO3 however existed, possibly totalling to a significant influence. To begin with there was a training session which may have made the task more familiar to the subjects and thus raised the overall level of evasion. More importantly, the worksheets were altered by adding an additional line. Whereas previous worksheets mentioned only the amount paid in taxes, the present ones also required the amount representing the 'correct' liability to be copied down. We believe that this addition may well have had the effect of drawing subjects' attention to the *difference* between the amount paid in taxes and the 'correct' liability when completing the tax form.

In comparison with NL02 a significant effect for the opportunity factor emerged for a different dependent variable, namely amount in guilders. In NL02 it was the frequency which appeared to have been affected. Again, we cannot be sure about the reason for this difference. It might have been an effect of the training session, in which items other than in the actual simulation were deductible. Another explanation, which we favour, is based on the difference in manipulations of the opportunity variable.

Where NL02 represented a clear-cut situation with regard to the exact nature of the itemised deductions, a different situation existed in NL03 for the subjects in the low-opportunity condition. In this condition the three deductions were randomly drawn from six alternatives. So situations may have occurred in which subjects had spent money on acquiring information, on advertising and improvements, and subsequently, when completing the tax form, then discovered that only one or two or even none of their deductions was allowed.

This may have caused a sense of unfairness in subjects, leading them to decide to overstate their deductions. This instigation may have well been equally strong in both opportunity conditions for that matter; there was no difference between the means of both opportunity conditions. The amount of evasion, however, may have followed the path we expected it to follow. A further point is that overstating on all six deductions would lead to a score of '1' on the evasion index. Thus the difference between subjects who overstated on only one or on all six deductions is not reflected in the index. On the other hand, the amount not reported is capable of reflecting these nuances as it simply adds up all constituent parts (we are assuming that more deduction deviations lead to a higher amount of evasion).

4.6 NL04: Decision frames and opportunity

There are several differences between this and the previous experiment, NL03. As a more or less general rule, tax-evasion simulations have relied on convenience samples of college students as subjects. For testing out procedures, this may be appropriate. However, as it is our aim to explore the correlates and determinants of tax-evasion behaviour of *regular* taxpayers, ideally it is this group one should study. Although selecting a sample may prove more cumbersome, the potential pay-offs in terms of the value of the results and the possibility of generalising the findings to the 'real' world are immense.

Method

Subjects   From adult education courses in Rotterdam and the local tele-phone directory, 85 members of the general public were recruited, 47 females and 36 males, with two persons not stating their sex on the questionnaire. Ages ranged between 21 and 75. Forty-seven of the subjects indicated that they had no experience with filing income-tax returns.

Design   As above, but with a change in the tax-declaration phase. To facilitate the effect of the withholding manipulation, participants were confronted with the amount of taxes due for refund or additional payment after completing the tax return. They could then review or alter the tax return as they wanted before 'filing' it. A direct result of this change was that subjects could determine the balanced amount as they altered the numbers in the tax form.

Procedure   Participants were invited to the university's premises at one of several specified time slots, distributed across the daytime and evening. After the simulation, a computerised measurement of individual social orientation was administered (Liebrand 1984). According to the scores on this instrument, subjects were classified as altruistic, cooperative, individualistic, or competitive. A postexperimental questionnaire measuring demographics, attitudes, and personality scales was also administered (see Table 4.11). Identical quantitative measures as in the previous simulations were ob-tained. A gift voucher of 25 guilders was presented to the participants as a token of appreciation.

Results

As in the previous simulations, we observed more cases of deduction fraud than of income fraud (47 versus 25 cases). Table 4.8 depicts the results of the 2×2 analyses of variance performed on the criterion variables with opportunity and decision frame as factors. A significant effect emerged for the opportunity factor on the frequency of evasion ($F = 5.3$, $p < 0.05$) and for the amount evaded in guilders ($F = 7.6$, $p < 0.01$). No significant effects were found for the decision-frame variable. Table 4.9, however, presents data that show that decision frame had the intended effect for those subjects who perceived the refund as a gain or the additional payment as a loss. The contrast for the amount reported is significant at $p = 0.051$.

Discussion

The results showed satisfactory results for the opportunity variable on both dependent variables. More importantly, the effect of the withholding variable is contrary to expectations. We find this disturbing; however, the manipu-lation checks have shown that only half of the people assigned to each

Table 4.8. *Mean number of times (out of 4) that taxes were evaded and amount in guilders not reported (in brackets) as a function of opportunity and decision frame (N=85)*

	Decision frame		
	Received refund	Made payment	Overall
Low opportunity	0.69 (9,201)	0.47 (1,665)	0.58 (5,555)
High opportunity	1.45 (36,573)	1.19 (20,574)	1.30 (27,092)
Overall	1.00 (20,352)	0.84 (11,425)	0.91 (15,581)

Table 4.9. *Mean number of times that taxes were evaded and amount in guilders not reported (in brackets) as a function of perceived decision frame*

Decision frame	
Gain	Loss
0.82	1.16
(6,705)	(27,386)
N = 17	N = 19

withholding condition perceived their situation as intended. This may easily have led to a different interpretation of the experimental situation, as subjects may have reacted to stimuli other than just the manipulations.

4.7 UK10 and UK11: Decision frames and opportunity

These British simulations represent replications of NL04. Slight changes were introduced in the text so as to tailor them to specific and local requirements. More importantly, two sets of subjects were recruited consecutively, a general-public sample and a student one. As the experiment for both groups was identical, and to simplify the presentation and discussion, we treat these groups as one data set.

Subjects　Seventy-two members of the general public were recruited, and 59 students. Students' ages ran from 18 to 30, and 36 females and 23 males participated. Only six of the students indicated they had experience with

Table 4.10. *Mean number of times (out of 4) that taxes were evaded and amount in £ sterling not reported (in brackets) as a function of opportunity and decision frame (N = 131)*

	Decision frame		
	Received refund	Made payment	Overall
Low opportunity	0.58 (2,400)	1.35 (9,472)	0.94 (5,720)
High opportunity	0.96 (6,265)	1.04 (3,981)	1.00 (5,056)
Overall	0.76 (4,255)	1.18 (6,507)	0.97 (5,381)

income-tax returns. Experience was more prevalent in the general-public sample, where 26 people indicated they had filed a tax return. Ages ranged from 23 to 62, with both sexes equally distributed among participants.

Design   The design and the manipulations were identical to the ones described in NL04. Some minor differences existed, most of which are due to 'hardware' factors. The Dutch experiments were run on personal computers with monochrome monitors, whereas the present simulations were implemented on BBC microcomputers attached to colour screens. Moreover, the English experiments did not contain a training session, which was used in the Dutch investigations solely for the purpose of familiarising the subjects with the task in hand (in previous versions we used elaborate written instructions, in later versions a summary instruction card for the same objective). We feel that these variations have not violated the comparability of the Dutch and British experiments.

Procedure   After the simulation, a small postexperimental questionnaire was administered. This contained manipulation checks, attitude and personality characteristics measures (see Table 4.11). More importantly, semi-structured interviews were conducted with some of the general-public participants two weeks after the simulation. These covered subjects' evasion within and without the experiment (see chapter 5).

Results
The data collected were analysed using a $2 \times 2 \times 2$ analysis of variance with decision frame, opportunity to evade and type of sample as factors. The overall means for both samples of frequency of evasion are presented in Table 4.10, with income fraud and deduction fraud contributing about equally to the number of frauds in total (46 versus 39 cases). For both the opportunity and the decision-frame factor the results were in the expected direction, although only for the latter did a significant effect emerge on the frequency of

Table 4.11. *Correlations between frequency of tax-evasion behaviour, age, sex, and individual difference measures (N's are 85, 72, 88, and 59 respectively)*

Variables	General public samples		Student samples	
	NLO4	UK10	NLO3	UK11
Attitudes				
Income evasion	−0.13	0.37**	0.25*	0.42**
Deduction evasion	−0.07	0.23	0.03	—
Personality attributes				
Attitude towards law	−0.06	0.04	−0.06	0.16
Alienation	0.33**	−0.14	0.07	−0.05
Risk seeking	0.01	0.04	0.16	0.41**
Demographics				
Age	0.14	−0.07	0.11	0.27*
Sex (higher = male)	0.16	0.01	−0.13	0.29*

$^*p<0.05$
$^{**}p<0.01$
—: no information

evasion ($F = 4.2$, $p < 0.05$). The results for the opportunity factor are not in the expected direction for the payment condition, owing to an outlier effect. The pattern in Table 4.10 is similar for both groups, with students typically evading more often (mean for students = 1.41, mean for general public = 0.66, $F = 14.0$, $p < 0.001$). An additional analysis on the perceived decision frame did not reveal more interesting data.

4.8 Correlational analyses

Elffers, Weigel, and Hessing (1987) have clearly shown a distinctive pattern of correlations associated with individual difference measures like personality characteristics and attitudes towards various evasive acts. Summarising, Elffers, Weigel, and Hessing found personality measures to predict documented tax-evasion behaviour only, while attitudinal measures predicted self-reported behaviour only. It should not come as a surprise when we state that, ideally, we wanted to replicate their findings using our behavioural simulation measures as a criterion for tax evasion. Table 4.11 depicts the relationships that were found between tax evasion and a selected number of individual difference measures.

At first, the pattern of correlational results in the table seems somewhat confusing, as it is at variance with the findings of Elffers, Weigel, and Hessing (1987). We need to take a closer look at the individual variables. Overall, age seems to be positively associated with evasion behaviour, which indicates that older people tend to evade more often than younger people. Most other investigators reporting on this relationship have found the opposite effect. In three of the four studies we found that men evaded more often than women, an effect corresponding with most other empirical investigations. Although this is consistent with previous work, we are not sure about the meaning of this association. As several other factors may simultaneously vary with sex of respondent (like income, opportunity to evade, education, and fiscal experience) it is likely that this association simply reflects the relationship between these factors and evasion. When respondents' sex is included as a balanced factor in an experimental design, no systematic significant effects on fiscal behaviour are obtained (Weigel 1989, personal communication). In our experiments, only once did we have a balanced distribution of age and sex across the experimental conditions (in UK10). We are not sure whether this accounts for the somewhat mixed or unexpected results for these demographic variables. Additional systematic observations may improve our knowledge here.

Positive attitudes towards evasion behaviour in *real life* were more often than not associated with more frequent evasion in the simulations. This relation may well be the result of measuring behaviour and the attitude towards that behaviour almost simultaneously, since in this situation it is more likely that people will answer attitude questions in a way that makes them congruent with their behaviour. Separating the measurement of both variables leads to a nonsignificant correlation (UK07). Likewise, self-reported evasion behaviour in the experiment relates to these attitudes in a positive sense as well. Given that self-reported evasion and attitudes were measured almost simultaneously this is not very surprising. Typically, self-reported income and deduction fraud correlate with the corresponding attitudes between $0.2 \leq r \leq 0.4$, significant at least at $p = 0.05$. Again, the NL04 sample stands out as it obtains low correlations for these variables ($r < 0.12$, n.s.).

The results obtained for the individual difference measures do not approach the expected and desired pattern. We would argue that the correlations between individual differences and evasion are insignificant, both statistically and conceptually. We could try to explain why some variables associate with our dependent measure in some samples just because they fit in so nicely. But we believe that this would just be capitalising on chance effects. It is more appropriate to point out that the correlations are generally low and in some instances act only to indicate the usefulness of certain individual difference variables. The pattern seems to be that the supposedly less stable attitude measurements correspond rather clearly with evasion behaviour and that the more constant personality characteristics do not. There are a few comments we would like to make on this issue. First, the relevance of individual differences may be quite different in the real world to the experimental world our subjects were presented with. Outside the laboratory, personality characteristics will guide many behaviours in many situations. However, in the experimental world behaviour is governed by two strong factors – our independent variables, decision frame and opportunity. This leaves very few degrees of freedom for the influence of other variables. Furthermore, the possible effect of individual differences is restricted as the task at hand is not framed as an alienation or a risk-taking situation. We would conclude that our simulations represent an environment in which there is little opportunity for individuals to behave solely according to their internal predispositions and motivations. Instead we believe that their behaviour will be governed by the environment we created.

Second, the differences between regular taxpayers and the nontaxpaying students are both demographic and psychological. The latter differences in particular may well lead to a different interpretation of the situation by the members of the two groups. It is conceivable that as a result of experience, economic socialisation in a different time and a differential professional background, members of the taxpaying population have acquired a general view of the world that is more stable and has more nuances than that of students. That people's interpretation of the 'objective' situation can alter their evasive behaviour has been shown conclusively (Webley & Halstead 1986; Baldry 1987; our own studies). Thus we might expect samples with different interpretations to show different patterns of correlations between evasion and individual difference variables. At this point it is worth mentioning a recent study, in which evasion behaviour in a simulation of entrepreneurs and government officials was compared (Robben, Hessing & Elffers 1990). The authors showed that no significant differences existed between the two professional groups for the frequency of evasion. Additional analyses showed that for certain personality characteristics like alienation, attitude towards the law, personal versus community orientation, and attitudes toward evasion the members of the two groups did not differ. We think this supports our view that a more coherent sample with regard to age and work experience reveals fewer differences on the variables mentioned.

Third, by manipulating the independent variables we created four different cells in our experiments. One can think of these four environments as yielding different behaviours, as that is exactly our intention. By lumping together all these 'different' behaviours any relationship between evasion and individual differences may be distorted.

One final point is that the simulations reported in this chapter are considerably more sophisticated than those reported in chapter 3, and, perhaps more to the point, have much more successful manipulations. This means that direct comparisons of the patterns of correlations found is probably inappropriate.

4.9   Conclusions

The findings of the studies reported above and their implications will be discussed separately for each of the predictors, withholding and opportunity to evade. Previous studies in the tax domain have not generally supported prospect theory. To explain why we think this is the case we have to consider both people's behaviour in the business simulation and how people respond to hypothetical decisions.

Let us take hypothetical situations first. Van der Pligt (1986), in a series of studies, presented both students and members of the general public with a range of prospect-style decisions put in an everyday context. Whether these items were framed as a loss or a gain, people were cautious with them. Van der Pligt suggests that prospect theory may be restricted in its application to abstract decisions and that certainty may be valued much more with mundane decisions. He also points out that much previous research has taken place in a social vacuum. On this interpretation, the results of studies of hypothetical tax choices would be expected since in these studies people draw on their experience and habitual responses in making their decisions and are less influenced by framing.

This is plausible but we would like to propose an alternative interpretation. When making a choice between a certain and a risky alternative, one is also choosing between acting honestly and acting dishonestly. It is likely that people will want to present an image of themselves as honest and also want to regard themselves as honest. In everyday tax evasion (and, we would maintain, our simulation) people are able to regard their behaviour not as evasion (dishonest) but as clever, justified, or reasonable. This is more difficult to do when confronted with two stark alternatives. On this argument, people's responses to hypothetical tax decisions are as unreliable as other kinds of self-report in this area (Hessing, Elffers & Weigel 1988) as they are heavily influenced by self-presentational concerns.

We believe that this limitation does not apply to experimental studies. Participants have a high level of involvement and, in most cases, do not perceive what the experiment is about. This ensures that the effect of self-presentational concerns (at least as regards honesty) is minimised. Thus we believe that the experiments described in this chapter provide strong evidence that prospect theory does help explain some tax evasion.

The position with regard to opportunity is less clear cut. One might argue that opportunity exists *per se*, or that it is more accurately represented as the opportunity to cheat with a reduced risk of detection. Long and Swingen

(1988) discuss this distinction, and report that, at least in the United States, all taxpayers have an equal opportunity to cheat. In some sense this was true in our experiments, as all participants had the option of reporting a zero income when declaring income. In the later experiments, opportunity was handled by manipulating the opportunity to cheat and to escape detection. As described earlier, we chose to do that by presenting subjects with varying numbers of alternatives they could use to misrepresent deductions and by altering the verifiability of their income. This suggests that what we were really doing was manipulating detectability of evasion. Redefining opportunity as detectability is probably a good idea as this is how it has been typically operationalised in past survey work (e.g. Stalans, Smith & Kinsey 1989) and experimental research (e.g. our UK and NL studies; Robben, Hessing & Elffers 1990), as well as research based upon official statistics (e.g. Clotfelter 1983; Witte & Woodbury 1985; Long & Schwartz 1987; Dubin & Wilde 1988; Long & Swingen 1988).

In a broader context, the effects of opportunity to evade and decision frame may be further illustrated by findings of Robbens *et al.* (1990). They found, by using simulations identical to the ones described in NL03, NL04, UK10 and UK11, in Belgium, Spain, Sweden, and the United States of America, rather strong effects for both predictor variables on the regular dependent variables. Taking the perceptions of gain or loss of the 674 participants into account, the effects were even stronger. This shows that these independent variables have a general impact regardless of particular tax culture.

The policy implication with regard to the decision-frame variable is fairly straightforward. Essentially it is that there should be an increase in income tax withheld at source. This will lead to a situation where very many individual taxpayers can expect a refund. But this is not sufficient. Tax authorities need to ensure that the refund is seen as a gain by the taxpayer to reduce the motivation to misrepresent income or deductions at the individual level. Taxpayers expecting a refund every year, however, might change their fiscal reference point, with possible effects for the gain perception of this return. With regard to opportunity to evade, we think we have provided some evidence that opportunity causes evasion, and is not merely a rationalisation of that behaviour. In everyday terms this means that the options taxpayers actually have at their disposal (or perceive that they have) need to be reduced significantly. This would, for instance, mean that all income taxes are to be withheld at source or that deductions are not allowed, or both, and implies a considerable simplification of the tax system.

5   The subjects' view

5.1 Introduction

One of our aims in this book has been to demonstrate that experimental approaches have an important role to play in furthering our understanding of tax evasion. Earlier we were somewhat critical of previous experiments in this area: their purpose has been transparent, the dependent measures just a repetitious series of income declarations, and the participants have been students (and often economics students to boot). This means that the participants almost certainly approached each experiment as an optimising situation and this seriously compromises their experimental realism.

This view is not just based on an analysis of the procedures used in past experiments but also on the postexperimental interviews carried out by Webley and Halstead (1986). These showed that very few subjects saw the experiment as a tax situation. On the contrary, most subjects saw the experiment as a game and were keen to point out that they would not approach filling out a real tax form in the same way. This may have been partially the result of the use of a microcomputer: some subjects pointed out that computers tend to be associated with games and there were many comments about the graphic display of the tax man which seemed to provide excitement, amusement and frustration. But the most important reason for the experiment being seen as a game is undoubtedly the nature of the task. As one subject noted, if you had not underdeclared income it really did not matter whether you were audited or not and so the game would not be enjoyable to play.

That the experiments reported in this book have experimental realism is therefore of great importance, otherwise we are in the unfortunate position of casting stones from a rather vulnerable position in a glass house. Readers can judge for themselves the adequacy of the procedures used: here we will present two kinds of information which bear on the issue of experimental realism. These are an overview of results from postexperimental questionnaires which provide a broad but limited picture and a description of some postexperimental interviews which give a more detailed impression of how subjects perceived the experiments.

5.2 Postexperimental questionnaires

In all of the Dutch experiments and in UK10 and UK11 participants completed a postexperimental questionnaire. As well as manipulation checks, these included a few questions about the experimental situation. Three of these will be considered here: two involved simple ratings of the realism and interest of the experiment, whilst the other was an open-ended question about the purpose of the experiment.

The wording of these questions differed very slightly (but not materially) from one study to the next. These versions (from UK10 and UK11) are typical: 'How interesting did you find the experiment (be honest!)?', 'How realistic was the simulation? In other words, how much were the decisions you made like those you would really make if running a small shop?', 'Say, briefly, what you thought the experiment was about?' For the interest question participants had to ring one of four responses (very uninteresting, uninteresting, interesting, very interesting) whereas the realism question was a five-point scale anchored with the terms 'very unrealistic' (1) and 'very realistic' (5).

The mean ratings for realism and interest are given in Table 5.1. For 'realism' these are satisfactory, though not outstanding. Few participants felt that the experiment was 'very unrealistic' (the maximum was four, in NL01) and the modal response was 3. The English participants overall judged the experiment as more realistic than the Dutch, and the English general-public sample gave the highest ratings of all (this should be borne in mind when reading the following section on postexperimental interviews). One question asked in NL01 but not later studies gives some additional evidence. Participants were asked whether they would react differently in reality: 32 said that they would, 34 said that they would not. This suggests that the experiment was going some way to evoking the desired behaviour. We cannot, of course, put too much trust in any of these ratings and they probably give us information about mundane rather than experimental realism. But low ratings would have given us pause for thought.

The generally high ratings for interest (the overwhelming majority in all experiments rated the experiment as 'interesting' or 'very interesting') provides some, though not compelling, evidence that the experiment was involving. The ratings differ little from one study to the next.

The open-ended question gave more variable results. The responses revealed a wide range of interpretations. Some believed the focus was on individuals ('Your capability in organising and maintaining something', 'ability to relate factors to achieve an end-goal'), others that we were interested in economic behaviour in general ('risk-taking in business', 'factors involved in making profits'). However, these were simply coded as to

Table 5.1. *Mean ratings of realism and interest (1 = low, 4/5 = high)*

	Realism (5-point scale)	Interest (4-point scale)
UK10 (general public)	3.6	3.2
NL04 (general public)	3.1	3.0
UK11 (student)	3.4	3.1
NL03 (student)	3.2	3.2
NL02 (student)	2.9	3.2
NL01 (student)	3.1	n/a

Table 5.2. *The numbers of participants who guessed the real purpose of the experiments*

	Did not guess purpose	Guessed real purpose	Did not respond
UK10 (general public)	64	8	0
NL04 (general public)	79	4	2
UK11 (student)	42	17	0
NL03 (student)	76	9	3
NL02 (student)	67	0	2

whether participants had guessed the real purpose of the experiment. This meant referring to evasion or cheating: mentioning taxes alone was not enough. Thus a response such as 'to test individuals' views on marketing and how their background can influence their ideas on marketing. The experiment was probably also to see how much idea each person had on marketing and tax etc.' would be coded as not having guessed the purpose of the experiment. Table 5.2 gives a breakdown of the 'real purpose' question for the withholding studies reported in chapter 4.

These figures are encouraging. Generally speaking only a small percentage (8% of the general public, 12% of the students) report detecting the real purpose of the experiments. Given that they may guess at the end of the experiment (when it does not matter) or even after having completed some of the questionnaire, this is a reasonably low figure. The English rates are higher than the Dutch rates, which may reflect the difficulty of carrying out a series of experiments on evasion in a small city; it is certainly the case that suspicion in the Exeter student samples has increased over the years.

Overall the answers on the postexperimental questionnaires suggest that participants find the experiments interesting, reasonably realistic, and, in most cases, believe them to be about something other than tax evasion. This is probably about the best we can expect. For a more detailed picture we can turn to the postexperimental interviews.

5.3 Postexperimental interviews

The exclusive use of quantitative data in tax-evasion experiments tends to obscure the diversity of processes that underlie people's behaviour. Postexperimental questionnaires provide some information about the success of manipulations and whether participants perceived the purpose of the study, but their ability to give us the 'participant's view' is limited. Qualitative data, on the other hand, especially that gathered in nonthreatening situations, may give us some insights into how respondents construe the experimental situation and their behaviour in it.

It is important, however, that we are not naive about these accounts. Take the example of an individual who acts in a game in a way that is considered unacceptable in everyday life. If he is asked about his behaviour afterwards, he will almost certainly attribute it to the demands of the game rather than to enduring personal characteristics. In the board game of Diplomacy, for example, the fact that an individual betrays his allies will not be attributed by him to his intrinsic untrustworthiness, although his opponents may well have other ideas. The account of behaviour given is a justification as well as an explanation. This has led many researchers to distrust what their subjects tell them (e.g. Freedman 1969). Furthermore, accounts of experimental behaviour may also be affected by what Orne (1962) called 'the pact of ignorance' between subject and experimenter. This refers to the unwillingness of subjects to reveal that they have detected the real purpose of an experiment in case by so doing they ruin the study.

This suggests that subjects' comments should not be taken at face value. This does not means that they should be dismissed or treated as unreliable but that the reasoning behind them needs to be investigated. If a respondent says, for example, 'I evaded tax in the experiment because it was just a game', this needs to be explored further; would he cheat at bridge, which is after all just a game, cheat at patience, or what have you? He could be asked why cheating at games is acceptable and to explain why he does it when others do not. Note that the same proviso applies to people who say that they behaved as they would in 'real life'. Since this answer could be motivated by a desire to give the experimenter what he wants, it also needs to be explored further. They could be asked why they behaved as in real life and what exactly that means to them.

Although this kind of probing questioning might be ideal, in practice it is difficult to achieve. The problem is that it is potentially very threatening and respondents may get very defensive. In the interviews we report here our strategy was to probe as far as possible whilst still maintaining rapport and to minimise defensiveness by presenting the interview situation as one in which respondents were helping us by being as open as possible. To distance respondents from their own behaviour the interviews were not conducted immediately after the experiment. In addition, to undermine any 'pact of ignorance', the interviewer was a research assistant who stressed her independence from the project.

Forty-eight of the participants in UK10 were interviewed in their own homes two weeks after the experiment. The interview was introduced as follows: 'This interview is concerned with how people behave in experiments. We have some worries about how far we can use experimental evidence, from studies like the one you took part in, to explain everyday behaviour and we'd like you to help us. We'd like to know how you saw your behaviour in the experiment, how you account for it and what influenced you. And we are going to focus on two areas, pricing and filling in tax forms.'

The interview then followed a semistructured format. The following questions were covered and a range of probes used depending upon the respondents' replies:

> What were you doing when you were pricing your goods?
> How would you account for the fact that you chose a high (low) price
>   from the range?
> What lay behind this decision?
> When you have priced things in real life (e.g. second-hand things, jumble
>   sales) what lies behind your decision then?
> Do you see the experimental and 'real' behaviour as comparable?
> Why (Why not)?
> When you were filling in the tax forms what were you doing?
> In filling a form in real life what would you be doing? Are the
>   experimental and real behaviours as comparable?
> Why (Why not)?

The questions were not always in exactly the same verbal form and since some respondents provided answers to later questions in their earlier replies, some questions were not directly asked at all. It should be noted that, as some people do not see what they do when filling in tax forms as a decision, we deliberately did not talk about a decision to evade or not.

Our main concern was that people's behaviour in the experiment might not be comparable to their real-life behaviour, so we will concentrate on this issue. Thirty-five of the participants saw their pricing behaviour as comparable and forty-one saw their tax behaviour as comparable. In this interview this difference between pricing and taxes is illustrated nicely:

I. Do you see the experimental and real-life behaviour as comparable in any way?

S. Not directly, because with a shop you don't have the bargaining power, I think. In real life, when you're selling the one-off article, which is all I have ever done, you do get the bargaining power.

I. With the tax forms, what were you doing?

S. I was declaring absolutely and honestly all the profit that I made. I worked in the tax office for 2 years when I left school. I now work in a bank and there is no way that I would try and do anything than declare the full profit.

I. In real life then, you would be honest?

S. Yes, absolutely, straight down the middle. I'd never put anything on the tax form that I don't think I'm entitled to claim and I declare every penny of income.

I. Why?

S. Because honesty is the best policy. I've a brother who is a tax collector as well, and I know what happens if you don't.

I. Is it partly fear of the consequences?

S. No, I like to think that I'm an upstanding citizen of this country, so therefore I believe that's the right thing to do.

I. So when you were working on the computer, you carried those beliefs with you onto the computer?

S. Yes, I did.

This is fairly typical. When the pricing behaviour was not seen as comparable, it was generally because it was seen as too constrained by the experiment. Respondents said that usually they would take into account the condition of the goods, or that they would be more cautious in real life, or, in a couple of cases, that they had no experience of ever selling anything. But the replies of these two respondents suggest that the pricing task was a reasonable facsimile:

I. How did you price your goods?

S. I was tending to aim towards the higher level of the acceptable range . . . because it did mention in the introduction that it wasn't necessarily right to charge the lowest price. And also because I feel that in business, if you tend to ask a fairly good price for your product, as long as the product is good enough, you will tend to get it. There is a danger of underpricing in reality.

I. O.K. Do you think that that behaviour and your experimental behaviour are comparable?

S. Well, we've actually got our own small business, and the prices are a combination of working out the hours of labour involved and paying myself and the man and also seeing what the market will stand.

I. Is what you did in the experiment what you would do in real life?

S. Yes. But that is almost certainly so because we had just started our business so it was all very much in my mind.

I.   Do you think that the behaviour and your experimental behaviour are comparable?
s.   Yes, I think they are. Because one looks at one's competitors, and what one's . . . I do actually run a small shop, so one has to compare with what the shop down the road is selling its comparable product for.

Nearly all subjects claimed that they were honest with regard to taxes in both the experiment and in real life. What is interesting and important is that the factors producing that similarity were generally held to be the same. A large number of respondents referred to the risks of being caught; phrases like 'you get caught sooner or later', 'there are various checks in the system', 'it is a government body, it always has the upper hand in the long run', and 'you've only got to slip up once with the tax man and you've had it' occurred often. Associated with these were statements like 'it said on the screen that you could be caught, it was, by not telling the truth' and 'the thought [about the consequences] had occurred to me'. This is well illustrated by this extract:

I.   So in the experiment you were honest and in real life you say you're honest too. Why?
s.   Cos, that's just the way I am.
I.   So even . . .
s.   I suppose it is fear of being caught. If you start trying to fiddle things you get caught sooner or later.
I.   And in the experiment you had the same kind of fear?
s.   Yes. I mean, I was acting how I would act in real life.

The other common explanation for their behaviour was in terms of personality or morals. There were references to 'integrity' and 'my Christian faith' and 'being straight'. For many of these people there seemed to be no alternative but to declare the correct figures. As one respondent put it, 'Well in a tax return, you're supposed to declare certain facts and either a fact is a fact or it isn't.' Two respondents referred to their jobs (police officer, probation officer), saying that it was just not possible to be anything other than honest for professional reasons.

The cases where tax behaviour was different in the experiment are particularly interesting. This respondent said that she had 'cheated a bit . . . you know . . . trying to get away with it', and was asked why:

s.   Well a bit daring really. I probably wouldn't cheat in real life, but I claimed a bit to see if I could get away with it and get more profit. You know, I wouldn't do it really.

After an extensive description of her honest behaviour in real life, she finished by saying that 'it's more like a game, like you play monopoly . . . I knew nothing could happen. It was only on a computer.' Another respondent who had evaded tax in the experiment was a little less sanguine about his everyday behaviour: 'I would hope in real life I would have behaved slightly more honestly than I did in the game.' That people should deny the relevance of evasion in the experiment to their usual behaviour is fairly predictable. Less expected are the comments of those people who were honest in the experiment but felt they might not be in real life. Two respondents said that they anticipated that in the long term in real life they would learn the 'tricks of the trade' and be able to avoid tax, and seven in total were self-professed 'potential evaders' though honest in the experiment.

None of the respondents actually admitted evading taxes in real life, though several came close, describing themselves as 'fairly honest' or commenting that they would 'avoid tax'. This respondent was the most articulate of this group of 'near-evaders' and identifies an important limitation of our current approach:

> s.   I think this was where it was different from real life. Because the computer was giving me a figure and there was a figure which, to change, I would have had to deliberately choose some arbitrary figure, solely to evade tax, whereas in real life you're making decisions all the time and it's always a question, sort of . . .
>
> i.   Right, so if you had to fill in a tax form in real life, how do you . . .?
>
> s.   Well you're scrupulously honest with the results that you've got at the end of the year, yes. I would be. So I'm erring on the honest side. But, um, I think along the way you might forget a few things, or you might, sort of, justify a few things, as to why they weren't relevant.

This would have the effect, as this respondent said, of 'skewing everything towards the honest because you have to be deliberately dishonest'.

Ideally we would have liked all our participants to have been psychologically involved in the experiment and for our manipulations to have elicited comparable behaviour to their real-life counterparts. From the interviews it is clear that the level of involvement was high. Three examples illustrate this:

> i.   Do you see the experimental behaviour and real behaviour as comparable?
>
> s.   In that I priced it as I meant it. I didn't mess about. Serious like.
>
> i.   Right. So you think that in a real-life situation you'd have done the same.
>
> s.   Oh yes, I didn't come up just to press buttons. I wanted to see if I could do it.
>
> i.   You took it seriously?
>
> s.   Yes. That's why it took so long, trying to work it out. I'd have been there all night, I think. I like to think about things.
>
> s.   Maybe I took it too serious, I don't know, but I thought, that's the way to do it. I did it, as I thought I would. I was a lot more interested

when I saw the computer. If I'd got a lot of forms to fill in I'd have probably gone 'Oh hell, I can't be bothered with this.' I'd have gone tick tick tick tick just to get out of there. But as soon as I saw it was a computer, 'cos I hadn't known that before, I hadn't really, I wanted to get into it.

But, equally clearly, we did not succeed with all participants. For some, the task was too difficult ('I wasn't quite sure what I was doing', 'I don't know a lot about tax forms, to be honest, and I was just guessing a lot of it, I'm afraid') and for at least one person too obvious ('the experiment seemed to expect you to diddle tax'). The interviews are naturally very variable in quality; some individuals are forthcoming, even garrulous, whilst others are as unthinking in the interview as they appear to have been in the experiment. The questionnaire responses, on the other hand, are necessarily restricted but at least give some information about how the experiments were perceived by large numbers of people. Taking the two together we would conclude that our experiments hide the tax aspect successfully, are involving, and do have psychological realism.

6 Tax-evasion experiments: An economist's view

FRANK A. COWELL
London School of Economics

Tax evasion is an awkward subject for economists. It is of enormous potential importance in policy design and in the workings of fiscal systems. However, it is – by its very nature – extraordinarily difficult to quantify. Data from official investigation are hardly ever available and data from other sources may be suspect: if you could directly observe and measure a hidden activity, then presumably it could not really have been properly hidden in the first place. This fundamental empirical conundrum has beset much of the serious work on the subject over the last twenty years.

I start, then, from the position that, with this particular economic and social phenomenon, economists can do with all the help that they can get from beyond the boundaries of their own profession. Tax practitioners and those with research interests in the area of public finance have cause to be grateful for the new opportunities which have been opened up by Webley, Robben, Elffers, and Hessing. In particular the authors' work has drawn attention to fresh sources of information about the motives and behaviour of tax evaders and should prompt those outside their discipline to take seriously research methods which may hitherto have been unfamiliar.

Tax authorities usually guard well the information that would otherwise provide a valuable database for academic researchers; and one can well understand why. Considerations of taxpayer confidentiality, the desire to sustain a healthy dread of the unknown amongst potential violaters of tax law, or perhaps even the instinct for self-preservation by inept officials tend to reinforce the instinct for reticence by government departments. Whatever the reasons may be, few countries have chosen to follow the example of the US Internal Revenue Service in making available the results of investigations and audits carried out by the tax authorities in their attempt to uncover tax evasion. So it is particularly remarkable that the authors have managed to unearth the first of the two special data sources reported here. By obtaining the cooperation of the Netherlands Ministry of Finance they have produced a data set that combines the thoroughness of official investigation with evidence of personal motivation in a way that is, as far as I am aware, unique. In a field where a lot of what passes for data is of questionable value, this achievement deserves to be better known and to be emulated by researchers and tax authorities elsewhere.

Unfortunately, for the reasons that I have stated, it is unlikely that Webley *et al.*'s first type of data is likely to become widely available from other governmental sources. So it is appropriate to concentrate upon the second data source which the authors have exploited – the results of their experiments – since this sort of data could, in principle, be replicated almost indefinitely. It would seem that all that is needed is an adequate supply of research funds, plus, of course, an adequate supply of willing subjects. However, this oversimplification does the subject two injustices. First, it underplays the potential usefulness of the approach. Second, it ignores some of the complex issues which determine whether or not one is likely to get useful research material out of the experiment.

Now I am not sure that economists trust experiments. Scan the empirical literature on the behaviour of tax evaders – or for that matter on other branches of consumer behaviour – and you will find very little that is based on this type of data. Experiments appear to be used only in situations when all else is seen to fail. So, what are they for? Should we believe the results?

Given the difficulty of getting worthwhile tax-evasion data from elsewhere, experiments are obviously useful for filling in the gaps. However, I think they are worth more than that. Even if tax authorities were willing to make information readily available, and even if reliable interview data with tax evaders could be obtained, tax evaders' behaviour in any situation will probably have been substantially affected by circumstances that may be quite specific and which it may be extremely difficult to control. Running an experiment could help one to understand how persons might react in a controlled environment purged of influences from factors such as the particular fiscal institutions or the 'climate' of compliance in the country where they happen to live. Of course these influences are themselves an interesting subject for study, but can usefully be treated as a separate issue.

The environment of a simulated business game seems to me ideal for throwing light on the right sort of question and, if the participants enter into the spirit of the game, there appears to be every reason to believe the results. Embedding the tax-evasion decision within a plethora of other business decisions is probably a very good way of reducing the distortions that might arise if respondents become self-conscious about their responses on this one particular issue. However, despite the careful set-up, problems may remain, so that it becomes difficult to interpret the connections between the parameters of the experiment and the subject's responses. It is clear, in the present study, that the experimenters themselves have not always been happy with the outcome of their own experiments (pp. 78, 88). I share some of their disappointments, but for reasons that are probably rather different from theirs.

Table 6.1.

		Audit probability (*p*)	
		1 in 6	3 in 6
Severity of fine (*s*)	2 ×	50%	−50%
	6 ×	−16.67%	−250%
			Rate of return (*r̄*)

The main problem that I have with some of the experiments reported here concerns a simple matter of economic logic. Suppose a person is disposed towards tax evasion – not as a matter of principle (for example, social protest) or obsession (rabid hatred of tax officials), but just because he is not too bothered about social constraints and the like. He is looking after the interests of Number One; he is therefore interested in the money. If he knows (or believes that he knows) the penalty for evasion (a surcharge *s* on the amount of tax evaded) and the probability of investigation and conviction (a number *p*) then there is an elementary sum that he can do: on each dollar of tax that he evades he will gain $1 with probability $1 - p$ and lose $s with probability *p*. The expected rate of return (*r̄*) in this gamble is thus $1 - p - ps$. Consider the implied value of *r* that would have confronted the experimental subjects in the case reported on p. 51. We can express this in percentage terms as in Table 6.1. Observe the negative entries that appear in the second line of the table, where the severity of the fine is extreme. Now if people are in it for the money why would they evade tax at all if the expected rate of return is less than zero? Why did anyone 'evade' at all in this part of the experiment?

Unfortunately there appears to be no way of distinguishing between two possibilities: whether participants in the experiment were unaware of the rate-of-return implications, or whether they just decided – in the full knowledge of the odds in heavy penalties – to go ahead and underreport anyway. Each of these has intriguing implications.

Consider the second of these two possibilities. We know that there are situations (such as race-track betting) where people will go ahead and take a risk, despite knowing the adverse odds. But in this case it seems to suggest an astonishing degree of recklessness in individual behaviour – what are we to make of someone who willingly takes on a risk that has an expectation of a hundred-per-cent loss? In the case of financial decisions this is analogous to the purchase of an asset on which the prospective rate of return is such that you expect to lose all of your principal. Perhaps there is something about the tax-evasion set-up that induces behaviour that could be regarded as crazy in other risk-taking situations – but if so it completely undermines the conventional economic model of evasion behaviour, and it would be interesting to know more. It would have been useful if the experiment had been extended or followed up in a way that clarified why such anomalous behaviour occurred. For example, it would be interesting to have a detailed comparison of the responses of subjects in cases where the payoffs to evasion are fully known in advance (such as the above) with those where little or no prior information about audit probabilities and fines is supplied (such as in UK08 – p. 87).

However, the first possibility cited above – where the participants were simply unaware of the arithmetic logic – calls into question not only the validity of the economic model of tax-evasion decisions based upon expected utility, but the validity of other aspects of the simulations as well. If the subjects did not understand the financial consequences of the stated penalties and audit probabilities, one should perhaps be sceptical of the conclusion (p. 50) that increasing the audit probability will reduce evasion activity, but that severity of fine will have no discernible effect.

There is, however, a further possibility – that subjects knew what the stated rules of the game implied, but that they just did not believe the stated probabilities and penalties. There may have been a failure of perception or feeling of artificiality about the problem which meant that the subjects did not respond as they would have done in an analogous set-up in the real world. Something like this seems to have occurred over the issue of inequity (p. 68). If this is so, then clearly the design of experiments in the future will need to be modified. But how?

One possibility is to make the simulation set-up more complex. Whilst I concur with the point made by Webley and Halstead (1986) that experiments need to be made more sophisticated in order to contribute significantly to our understanding of tax evasion, I do not agree fully with the present authors in their similar conclusions on experimental methodology (p. 78), that participants in experiments should be able to evade in as many ways as they can in everyday life. I have two objections. The first is that making experiments more complicated may make them harder to interpret in any useful way. The second is that it simply cannot be done. The reason for this assertion is that tax evasion is, at bottom, about breaking the rules. Now, depending on the particular social and legal set-up in everyday life, people may choose to break the rules in certain well-specified ways – they underdeclare income, they overclaim on expenses – but it is unwise to suppose that all the possibly useful set of rule-breaking strategies can be encompassed within another set of rules, i.e. the rules of the experiment. In real life people will invent completely new ways of breaking the rules if they can. Admittedly economic modelling of tax evasion is prone to falling into a similar methodological trap (for example, a lot of work assumes that people either report honestly or dishonestly: but why assume that they make a report at all?); however, in my view that just restricts the applicability of the theoretical models and should not be taken as a guide for experimenters. It is tempting to think that experimental design can be made richer and more lifelike by switching from a game of draughts to a game of chess; but this may not be of much practical advantage if, in real life, people just kick over the chessboard.

On the other hand, the careful approach of the authors in their sequence of experiments prompts a couple of suggestions for further development of experimental models of this kind. The first is to make more explicit the two-stage nature of the decisions that are being taken. It would be potentially very useful if the set-up of future experiments and the processing of the results could be set up in such a way as to clarify (1) the factors which predispose individuals as to whether they will obey or break the rules about paying taxes, and (2) amongst those who do break the rules the (possibly different) factors which influence by how much they underreport or overclaim.

Secondly, following up the experimental session with some sort of 'what did you think you were doing at the time' questioning (chapter 5) seems to add enormously to the value of the experiment. To some extent it offsets the unease felt by many about a fundamental issue in the experimental approach to investigating economic behaviour: the problem that the subjects' awareness that they are in an experiment substantially alters the nature of their responses.

Nevertheless, even if future work does not include these refinements, the body of evidence which has been assembled by the authors has provided a valuable service to economists and others. It has helped us to know something about that which might otherwise be unknowable.

7 The conduct of tax-evasion experiments: Validation, analytical methods, and experimental realism

SUSAN LONG and JUDYTH SWINGEN

Syracuse University, Center for Tax Studies and Rochester Institute of Technology

Tax evasion is a complex and generally hidden behaviour which can have significant social and economic consequences. In recent years, researchers from a wide variety of disciplines have sought to understand why we do or do not pay taxes, what types of individuals and/or transactions are prone to evasion, and the true extent of taxpayer noncompliance. The series of experiments reported in this monograph make a notable addition to this literature. The purpose of this chapter is to comment on these experiments and suggest extensions, highlighting some of the important contributions this experimental work makes.

The chapter is divided into two main sections. The first section discusses some methodological questions relevant to validation and model testing. It outlines some further approaches to analysing these data which might help account for certain patterns in outcomes across experiments, as well as provide additional insights into the dynamics of tax-evasion behaviours. These extensions, we suggest, would result in a fuller examination and test of the authors' theoretical framework.

The second section of this chapter offers some personal reflections on these experimental findings, drawing upon what we know about the US tax-setting and taxpayer-compliance patterns. We note that distinctions between tax evasion vs. tax noncompliance and between tax evasion and avoidance are critical not only in estimating the extent of tax evasion, but in adequately modelling the decision processes. The chapter concludes with some implications of these distinctions for the design of future tax-evasion experiments.

7.1 Some methodological issues in the analysis of experimental data

A major strength of this monograph is that it describes research which in fact does what we so often say SHOULD be done for good science, but then FAIL actually to do. Four particular elements of their research strategy are particularly noteworthy: its cross-disciplinary *and* cross-cultural scope, the emphasis on the importance of replication, its thoughtful treatment of null

128

findings, and the careful attention given to *external* validity in the design and execution of the experiments. There are several additional issues relevant to validation of the experimental implementation and to model testing which were given less attention. It is to an examination of two of these that we now turn.

7.1.1   Random assignment and equivalent groups

Experimental designs control assignment to comparison groups to help ensure that the makeup of the groups are alike. But experimental designs do not guarantee equivalence. It is a common misperception that randomly assigning individuals to treatment and control groups – the procedure used in the experiments discussed in the earlier chapters – ensures equivalence for the experiment. This is not so.

What is true is that if the same experiment were run many many times the average characteristics of the different comparison groups would be the same. In the short run, and in particular in any short series of experiments, equivalence is not assured even with large experimental groups. With random assignment, chance variations can result in the characteristics of the comparison groups being substantially different. Thus, it is always advisable to assess empirically whether random assignment has resulted in equivalent groups.

The researchers did take particular care in validating the implementation of the experimental design in a number of important ways. Postexperimental questionnaires were filled out, and open-ended personal interviews of a number of subjects were conducted. But little attention seems to have been given to the question of equivalence. As has been common in other tax-evasion experiments, random assignment of individuals across experimental conditions was simply assumed to have resulted in comparable groups.

Two specific aspects of these experiments, however, make the equivalence assumption troublesome. First, a relatively small number of subjects – from a low of 2 to 22 – were used for each comparison group. Second, a feature of these experiments was the variability of subjects' responses, reflecting variability in the distribution of some key characteristics in the subject pool used. There was a substantial proportion of subjects who did not respond to any of the experimental manipulations and always reported income accurately. The authors noted that almost two thirds of their subjects (64%) in one experiment (NL02) did not evade at any point during the experiment. For many of the other experiments, about half evaded and half did not, and only in two experiments did the proportion who never evaded drop as low as one-quarter to one-third. This variability did not seem to be related to the experimental conditions, but rather reflected the particular subject pool used.

The existence of significant numbers of subjects who never evade has also characterised many experiments in tax evasion in the US (see, for example, Alm, Jackson & McKee 1988; Beck, Davis & Jung 1989; Alm, McClelland & Schulze 1989). Some individuals are simply predisposed NOT to evade. Where a substantial proportion of subjects are of this predisposition, the *distribution* of these 'honest' subjects across experimental cells can have a dramatic impact on results. The frequency of evasion in experimental cells which have disproportionate numbers of 'honest' subjects could significantly depress observed evasion rates; likewise experimental cells with fewer numbers of honest subjects would be expected to have above-average evasion scores. Thus, observed patterns of evasion could be substantially distorted (both up and down), masking true experimental effects.

How often should significant distortions arise? Surprisingly often, as can be seen in Table 7.1, which summarises a series of probability experiments we conducted. The probability of *substantial* departures from equivalence rises as there are: (1) fewer subjects per experimental group, (2) a larger number of groups being compared, or (3) greater variability in the characteristics of the subject pool.

As shown in Table 7.1, if a quarter of all subjects are predisposed against evasion, and there are two subjects per comparison group, then the odds are less than half (46%) that any two comparison groups will have the same proportion of honestly predisposed subjects, and only 12% for any four comparison groups. When half of all subjects are predisposed to be honest, this increased variability reduces the odds of exact equivalence even further.

As sample sizes increase, the odds of *exact* equivalence also decrease. With 20 subjects, for example, there is only a 15% chance that any two groups will have the same composition, and only a remote chance (less than 0.5%) that any four groups will have the same makeup. But larger sample sizes do reduce the likelihood that the differences which occur will be *substantial.* However, sample sizes of 10 or even 20 per experimental group may still not be large enough. For example, the odds are still 50/50 (for $N = 20$) and over 75/25 (for $N = 10$) that any three groups will differ in composition by at least 20%. These odds are even less favourable as the number of comparison groups grow.

With this degree of variation in the likely makeup of the experimental cells, it is always important to check that random assignment has resulted in comparable groups for any given experiment. Instead of analysis of variance, an analysis of covariance design may be more appropriate. Such designs have the added advantage, even when groups are comparable, of reducing unexplained error variance and thereby adding power to the experimental tests.

Rather than applying a statistical fix-up after the fact, a better plan is to use either substantially larger sample sizes for each experimental cell or to stratify subjects on important characteristics and randomly assign subjects to experimental cells within these strata. Only this latter approach assures exact equivalence on those characteristics. This was the approach employed in a number of the earlier experiments to ensure equal distribution of males and females across experimental cells.

For tax-evasion experiments, this type of stratified random assignment strategy may be difficult to implement for some important characteristics. For example, predisposition against evasion and risk preferences may be difficult to ascertain reliably beforehand. Or the questions administered at the time of assignment to elicit this information can be reactive (Webb *et al.* 1966) – that is, influence the later behaviour of subjects during the experiment by sensitising them to particular features such as honest versus dishonest reporting, or the risks of detection. But, given the potential impact of nonequivalence on the outcome of the experiment, greater attention in tax-evasion experiments must be given to minimising these sources of potential experimental error.

7.1.2   *Exploiting within-group and cross-time variation in evasion behaviours*

What key characteristics might be used to stratify subjects when randomly assigning them to experimental groups? The authors used gender to stratify subjects before random assignment in many of these experiments. While behavioural differences related to gender have been noted in some past research, few were found in these experiments. An analysis of correlates of evasion behaviour in these data – particularly those which explain variation within treatment groups, or interact with treatment effectiveness – can help isolate useful stratification variables for future research.

However, this is not the only reason why an examination of variation around group means in these experiments can be valuable. A basic justification for any such inquiry is to try to understand why people react differently to the same stimuli.

The factors – situational and psychological – identified by the theoretical framework adopted by the authors (Weigel, Hessing & Elffers 1987) were seen not only as important causes of tax evasion but as (p. 22) 'sufficient to explain evasion.' A full model test would thus examine not only how successful the experimental manipulations of situational factors were in altering behaviour between cells, but whether variation within cells can be accounted for by the psychological factors posited in this theory. In designing such a test several considerations should be kept in mind. First, since the Weigel, Hessing, and Elffers theory involves multiple psychological factors, multivariate – not bivariate – tests are required. Whether or not a factor has a statistically significant bivariate correlation with tax evasion, as was

Table 7.1. *The probability in percentages that random assignment in experimental settings results in comparison groups with identical vs. different compositions*

	Proportion of subject population predisposed not to evade*								
	0.10			0.25			0.50		
	Number of comparison groups			Number of comparison groups			Number of comparison groups		
	2	3	4	2	3	4	2	3	4
				2 subjects per group					
Exact equivalence:	69%	54%	43%	46%	23%	12%	38%	16%	7%
Groups differ by at least:									
50%	31	46	57	54	77	88	63	84	93
100%	2	3	4	7	15	21	13	28	43
				4 subjects per group					
Exact equivalence:	52	31	19	32	12	4	27	8	3
Groups differ by at least:									
25%	48	69	81	68	88	96	73	92	97
50%	7	13	19	21	41	57	29	53	70
75%	—	1	1	4	8	13	7	17	27
100%	—	—	—	—	1	1	1	2	4
				10 subjects per group					
Exact equivalence:	31	11	4	21	5	1	18	4	1
Groups differ by at least:									
10%	69	89	96	79	95	99	82	96	99
20%	24	45	61	43	71	85	50	78	90
30%	6	13	20	19	39	55	26	50	67
40%	1	2	4	7	16	26	12	26	39
50%	—	—	—	2	5	8	4	10	17
60%	—	—	—	—	1	2	1	3	6
70%	—	—	—	—	—	—	—	1	1

			20 subjects per group						
	21	5	1	15	2	—	13	2	—
Exact equivalence:									
Groups differ by at least:									
5%	79	95	99	85	98	100	87	98	100
10%	42	69	84	58	84	94	64	88	96
20%	6	14	23	20	40	57	27	51	68
30%	—	1	2	4	11	18	8	19	30
40%	—	—	—	1	2	3	2	4	8
50%	—	—	—	—	—	—	—	1	1
60%	—	—	—	—	—	—	—	—	—
70%	—	—	—	—	—	—	—	—	—

— means less than 0.5%

*Results are symmetric so that values tabulated for a proportion of 0.10 apply equally to a proportion of 0.90, and values tabulated for a proportion of 0.25 apply equally to a proportion of 0.75

examined by the authors, is not a valid guide since either the absence of a correlation or its strong presence can be entirely spurious – the result of the failure to control for other factors posited by the theory. Secondly, if attitudes mediate the impact of social conditions on actual evasion behaviour (see p. 22), then the impact of the experiment on subjects' behaviours depends in part on their psychology. Thus, an interactive, rather than an additive, model should be used for the analysis. Third, in any fuller test of the authors' theory which seeks to explain variation of response within as well as across experimental conditions, the common assumption that the frequency (or size) of misreporting can be usefully modelled as a simple continuous variable may not be appropriate. This continuity assumption implies that the causal forces which explain why an individual does or doesn't misreport his or her taxable income are identical to those which account for whether an individual engages in 1 versus 2, or 7 versus 8 acts of evasion.

However, moving from not evading to evading resembles crossing a threshold; the forces which determine which side of the threshold a person decides to be on may differ from those which, once this threshold is passed, determine behaviour on the other side. For example, moral beliefs about the propriety of evasion may help determine whether an individual engages in evasion behaviour, but once the initial evasion occurs such beliefs may no longer function as an effective constraint on the frequency of subsequent evasion. Once individuals begin to evade they may rationalise that this behaviour is acceptable, using logic such as: 'everybody cheats a little', or 'the tax system is unfair and I have already paid my fair share'. In this case, evasion behaviour reflects not a single decision but a series of decisions (Smith & Kinsey 1987). One decision model may be needed for explaining whether or not a subject engages in any evasion behaviour, and a somewhat different model used to account for the extent of evasion. While it is likely that a number of variables will be common to both models, their relative influence may differ in each. Also, the approach required to represent a choice model needs to be appropriate for the dichotomous dependent variable (evade/not evade) involved.

Finally, to understand subjects' evasion behaviours it may be useful to add a temporal component to the analysis. Individual evasion behaviours can be classified not only on their frequency or magnitude, but on the consistency of this evasion behaviour across trials. To what extent did behaviour (evasion or compliance) on the first round persist? Once the subject evaded, did this behaviour continue across subsequent rounds, or do some subjects move in and out of evasion almost at random? Some attention in the earlier experiments was given by the authors to the timing of the audit, but this and other temporal issues were not systematically pursued. If, as the authors note, evasion behaviour should be understood not as an act but a process, then more attention to these temporal patterns seems warranted.

7.2   Reflections in the light of US experience

A major strength of these experiments is the new vehicle – the business simulation – the authors have devised for significantly strengthening external validity in tax-evasion experiments. In this section, drawing upon what we know about the US tax setting and features of American tax compliance, we offer some personal reflections on some of the new possibilities this approach opens for future experiments. We begin with basic definitional matters, and their implications for the design of future tax-evasion experiments.

7.2.1   Tax avoidance and evasion as substitute behaviours

In the real world, those who wish to reduce their income-tax liability have more choices than just tax evasion. In most countries, there are many perfectly legal 'tax avoidance' strategies for arranging financial affairs to minimise taxes. Indeed, the promotion of tax shelters and other tax-avoidance strategies has been a major growth industry. In reaction, recommendations for legislative change to restrict these activities has surfaced in many countries. (See, for example, recommendations of the Lord Keith Committee inquiry, 1983, in Great Britain, proposals of the Oort Commission, 1986, in the Netherlands, and legislative proposals in the United States which were incorporated in the Tax Reform Act of 1986.)

These tax-avoidance strategies can often provide attractive alternatives to tax evasion. However, the experiments discussed in this monograph (along with most past experimental studies) frame the taxpayer's decision as a choice between two alternatives: honest-versus-dishonest reporting. If reduction of tax liability was desired, the subject's choice was limited to that of evasion.

Given the importance of framing demonstrated in this research, a useful extension for future experimental investigation would be to expand the choices the taxpayer faces to include tax-avoidance strategies. A theoretical paper by Alm (1988) suggests that the addition of an option to avoid rather than evade taxes had a substantial impact upon model predictions concerning evasion (see also, Cross & Shaw 1982; Alm, Bahl & Murray 1989).

Since in the real world the degree of opportunity afforded for tax avoidance is dependent in part upon having sufficient disposable assets or income available to invest, setting up an analogous experimental situation where tax avoidance opportunity is manipulated might also present an alternative vehicle for experimentally manipulating perceived inequity of the tax system to see if the null results that the authors found in chapter 3 can be replicated. Further, it would also allow a direct test of the often repeated assertion that the availability of these so-called 'tax loopholes' to the rich undermine the average taxpayer's willingness to comply (see Swingen 1989; McKee & Gerbing 1989).

7.2.2   Tax noncompliance versus tax evasion

The authors properly point to the very different coverage of behaviours encompassed by the terms tax noncompliance (referring to any mispayment of taxes) versus tax evasion resulting from an 'intention to defraud the authorities' (p. 2).

There are equally important distinctions over the potential penalties for these different acts. In particular, tax evasion is defined in the United States as a criminal behaviour, and carries with it not only the threat of criminal prosecution, but on conviction a good likelihood of being sent to prison (over 50% in the US, see Long 1980, 19). In contrast, tax noncompliance without intent to evade is handled administratively and the fact that tax misreporting has occurred is held strictly confidential. If sanctions are administratively imposed they are limited to financial penalties. The more typical result is simply to require payment of back taxes with interest.

Tax-evasion experiments have generally failed to incorporate these distinctions. There is no threat of public exposure as a tax evader or any risk of prosecution and imprisonment. Penalties are limited to financial ones, largely administered privately. Even the method of calculating the penalty, proportional to the tax amount not reported, resembles how many civil penalities are calculated in the US. In contrast, a maximum dollar amount is set by statute in the US for criminal fines, and the amount imposed need not bear any relationship to the amount of taxes evaded.

These criticisms are not meant to invalidate tax-evasion experiments or the internal validity of their results. But they raise some interesting issues concerning the generalisability of these results to actual tax evasion – especially in those countries which treat tax evasion as a criminal offence.

In defence of the current focus on financial penalties in tax-evasion experiments, it seems that the risk of criminal prosecution for tax evasion in most countries is not high – in part because it is easier to slap a financial penalty on the evader administratively than bring a criminal prosecution (see Long 1981). For example, in England only about 25 prosecutions are made annually for false income-tax returns (Smith 1986). In the United States, the level of criminal prosecutions, while higher, is still quite low – in 1988, 2,491 individuals were convicted of tax crimes by the federal government, and even this figure encompasses a much broader scope of offences than just income-tax evasion (IRS 1989). None the less, whatever the objective odds of criminal prosecution, the risk is still very real and is heightened because many taxpayers tend greatly to overestimate the real risks.

Some might argue that it is not the nature of the penalties (financial versus corporal), but their magnitude that matters. We would disagree. Substituting one type of penalty for another in an experimental test would clearly be expected to have different effects for different individuals. For those that have strongly internalised moral beliefs about the impropriety of evasion – the third personal constraint on the Weigel-Hessing-Elffers framework – the threat of any external penalty may be unnecessary to be deterred. For others, as Vogel (1974) suggests, the stigma of being labelled a tax evader would be a much more effective deterrent than having to pay even a very large financial penalty. For some, the prison term would impose the greatest hardship, while still others would be most deterred perhaps through heavy financial penalties. Thus, depending upon the specific type of penalty, the associational pattern of evasion behaviour with different social and psychological conditions might indeed be quite different.

Are empirical tests for a differential impact of separate types of tax penalties possible? Can tax-evasion experiments be devised which operationalise criminal penalties in such a way as to engage the 'same psychological processes as their real-world counterparts' (p. 45)? This seems difficult, both because of the limitations in time and space, and the need to protect human subjects from potentially harmful pressures. One could evict those caught cheating from participating in the rest of the experiment as the analogue of removing evaders from society by putting them in prison, but it is difficult to believe that the result would be anything close to psychologically analogous. Socially stigmatising evaders could no doubt be done, but whether this could be accomplished in an ethical manner is debatable. However difficult it may be to come up with an acceptable implementation of criminal sanctions within a laboratory setting, unless (or until) this is done, results may not be generalisable to real-world settings where the threat of criminal sanctions for tax evasion (including incarceration) occurs.

7.2.3 The impact of complexity and opportunity on taxpayer compliance

Finally, the experiments reported in the earlier chapters present taxable income to the subjects as a known number. In the United States, legal ambiguities real or perceived, the quality of a taxpayer's records, and the nature and volume of a taxpayer's transactions make calculating taxable income less clear cut. This seems also to be the case in other western countries, particularly for business taxpayers. As one of the subjects in their experiments commented, it is this character of the tax-reporting process itself which may influence the decision to noncomply (p. 121):

> s. I think this was where it was different from real life. Because the computer was giving me a figure and there was a figure which, to change, I would have had to deliberately choose some arbitrary

figure, solely to evade tax, whereas in real life you're making
decisions all the time and its always a question of, sort of . . .

I.   Right, so if you had to fill in a tax form in real life, how do you . . .?

s.   Well you're scrupulously honest with the results that you've got at
the end of the year, yes. I would be. So I'm erring on the honest side.
But, um, I think along the way you might forget a few things, or you
might, sort of, justify a few things, as to why they weren't relevant.

Tax-evasion experiments by the relative simplicity of the reporting task do
not provide subjects with opportunities to hide their evasion (either to the tax
authorities or to themselves) under the guise of an 'honest mistake' or as a
'reasonable difference of opinion' when interpreting ambiguous or uncertain
tax requirements. Thus, when tax authorities detect that misreporting
occurred, they still may not detect that it was tax evasion which was
intended. This important distinction between these two types of detectability
is not preserved in the typical laboratory experiment.

Because many modern income tax statutes are quite complicated, and in
addition leave significant areas of uncertainty or ambiguity in tax requirements, mistakes are common. Separating out those which are truly 'honest
mistakes' from those that aren't is often not possible. Thus, while complicated
tax laws make it more difficult and burdensome for the honest taxpayer to
comply, they provide convenient excuses for the dishonest to hide behind
which minimises their risks of incurring criminal sanctions, and may also
provide evaders with what they may convince themselves is adequate self-
rationalisation for their own behaviour.

The built-in assumption that taxable income is a known number in these
tax-evasion experiments may have reduced not only the overall incidence of
evasion behaviour, but changed its distribution across subjects. The
innovative approach to evasion experiments within a business simulation
that the authors have pioneered, however, could be readily adapted so that
taxable income is not such a clear-cut number.

While incorporating more realism into the experimental tax-reporting task
would be relatively straightforward in a business-simulation framework,
analysing the results for their implications about tax evasion would not be.
Adding realism here adds complexity. This complexity could be expected to
produce a higher volume of unintentional errors (see, for example, Robben *et
al.* 1990) which would need to be removed before experimental effects on tax
evasion could be isolated. This might be achieved by observing the baseline
level of errors when no evasion incentives are present against the level when
incentives for evasion are experimentally introduced.

Each of these new directions for additional laboratory research, using ever
more realistic experimental settings, could shed important new light on the
determinants of tax-evasion behaviour, as well as on tax-compliance
behaviours more generally.

8 Reply and conclusions

We hope that the two commentaries have had the same effect on the reader as on ourselves: they have made us reconsider some implicit assumptions, encouraged some anxious soul-searching about appropriate forms of analysis, and provoked hours of heated discussion. We do not intend to defend our position tooth and nail: we agree with much that our commentators have said and accept that there are limitations in the designs and the analyses of our experiments. Rather, we wish to contribute to a forward-looking debate (whilst at the same time indulging in a rearguard defence of some of our decisions). To that end we will discuss three issues: the expected return of evading taxes, the existence of hard-core nonevaders and the problem of complexity, and finish with a few concluding remarks.

8.1 The expected return of evading taxes

The main difficulty that Cowell has with some of our experiments is a matter, as he puts it, of simple economic logic. The matter is not, for us at least, simple (the wastepaper baskets full of scrumpled calculations bear mute witness to this fact). The basic problem is that the expected rate of return of evading taxes in certain experimental conditions in two of our experiments is less than zero. This is true for three of the four conditions in UK04 and the conditions in UK05 (in all other experiments no exact information was given on audit frequency or fine rate).

Cowell suggests that there are three possible explanations for this: that participants were unaware of the poor odds and evaded tax anyway, that participants were unaware of the economic logic, or that they just did not believe the stated probabilities and penalties. If either the first or third of these explanations is accurate it would be extremely worrying. We would probably have to conclude that the external validity of these experiments was doubtful since participants were being foolhardy or sceptical in a way that does not correspond to everyday behaviour. However, we favour the second explanation.

The reason for this is rather embarrassing, but confession is supposed to be good for the soul. In designing UK04, PW assumed (wrongly as it turns out) that an audit probability of 1 in 2 coupled with a fine rate of 2 times was mathematically equivalent to an audit probability of 1 in 6 coupled with a fine rate of 6 times. These were assumed to be neutral with an expected rate of return to zero. This is true only if paying a fine is an alternative to paying tax: if you have to pay a fine *and* the tax you should have paid for that period then the expected rate of return is negative.

In our experiments the second alternative applies. But the fact that the experimenter believed the rate of return to be neutral suggests that the participants may have made a similar mistake. This seems especially likely given that the instructions did not make the exact position clear.

Cowell claims that if participants were unaware of the economic logic then this calls into question the validity of aspects of the simulation. We simply do not accept this. It seems to imply that unless participants reason like economists we cannot take their behaviour too seriously. It seems more reasonable to assume that they attend to both fine rate and audit frequency but that, in this particular case, where audit frequency changed during the course of the experiment, audit frequency was more salient. On a more general level, we believe that it is precisely because participants often do act in ways that are counterintuitive or contrary to rational models that experimentation is worthwhile. Kahneman and Tversky's (1979, 1984) work is a good example.

8.2   The existence of hard-core nonevaders

Long and Swingen's lucid analysis of some of the methodological issues involved in the analysis of experimental data is simultaneously a corrective and a spur to future action. We will try harder in future. But we have our doubts about one of the planks of their critique, namely the existence of a hard-core of nonevaders.

Their claim is that 'some individuals are simply predisposed NOT to evade'. If this is true then it is indeed the case that the distribution of honest subjects across the experimental cells may dramatically alter the results. But what is the evidence that such people exist in any number?

Long and Swingen base their assertion on the fact that in most of our experiments a substantial proportion of individuals did not evade and that this is also true of American tax-evasion experiments. Furthermore, the variation in general levels of evasion across experiments was attributed by Long and Swingen to the subject pools used rather than to the differences in particular experimental conditions.

We would like to make four points about this. First, in our experiments people are tested only once. Although in the earlier experiments they made a number of tax declarations, in the later experiments they made only two. On this basis it is impossible to assert that people are hard-core nonevaders; it is necessary to test people repeatedly to see if they are genuinely consistent nonevaders. Second, it is possible that the differences in overall level of evasion found in different experiments do not reflect the nature of the subject pools used but differences in contextual factors, such as the exact recruitment procedure used, whether the participants were tested singly or in groups, the location of the experiment, the non-verbal behaviour of the experimenter, and so on. All of these may suppress or elevate the overall level of evasion. To say this does not invalidate our findings; it is simply a recognition that behaviour in an experiment is determined by many factors, some of which are outside the control of the experimenter. Third, replication of experiments effectively finesses the issue of nonrandom allocation. If this were a really serious problem we would not find, as we did in the studies reported in chapter 4, a consistent pattern of results. Fourth, and most important, the evidence from outside the experimental setting suggests that the hard-core nonevader is a chimera, or at the least a rather rare beast. For example, Isachsen, Samuelson, and Strøm (1985) report a survey of 700 Norwegian adults in which respondents were classified into four categories: moralist (those declining to participate in any form of tax evasion), passive/rationed (those considering the return on tax evasion not worthwhile or who wished to participate in the shadow economy but couldn't find work), partially active, and active. Only 15% of the sample were classified as 'moralists'. What is particularly interesting is that in modelling individuals' decisions to evade it made little difference whether this group was included or not. This led Isachsen, Samuelson, and Strøm to conclude that Norwegian 'true moralists' were very thin on the ground. Another survey, this time carried out in the Netherlands (Berghuis & Kommer 1984), suggests that only 20 to 25% of the population have no sympathy for evaders and that the overwhelming majority find it understandable. Given the likely biases in self-report, this also implies a rather low percentage of individuals who could not imagine evading under any circumstances.

If the proportion of the subject population that is predisposed NOT to evade is low then we can see from Table 7.1 that equivalence is not a serious issue. With a proportion of 10% and with ten subjects per group, most groups do not differ by more than 20%. To say this is not to minimise the problem, but just to put it in perspective. We share Long and Swingen's view that more attention needs to be given to dealing with these sources of experimental error. We are pessimistic, however, about the chances of stratifying samples on relevant characteristics since we have not had much luck in identifying relevant characteristics. The way forward may be to follow another of their suggestions and to exploit the temporal dimension; it would be an easy matter to get initial baseline information on evasion disposition by adding a premanipulation year or years.

8.3   Keep them simple?

It is interesting that our commentators have rather different views on the merits of more complicated experiments. Long and Swingen believe that complexity and realism will greatly enhance the power and applicability of tax experiments. Cowell, on the other hand, argues that making experiments more complex makes them harder to interpret. Furthermore, he claims that it is not possible to set up experiments where people can evade in as many ways as they can in everyday life, since 'in real life people will invent completely new ways of breaking the rules if they can'. Our feeling is that people can also invent new ways of evading in our experiments. In some of our early experiments (not reported in this book) some computer-literate participants listed the program in order to discover the 'rules of the game'. It is also common, if many people are participating simultaneously, for people to try to ask their neighbours for assistance. These behaviours were not used as dependent measures but there is no reason in principle why they should not have been. In our most recent experiment, as Long and Swingen point out, participants made a number of mathematical and clerical errors. These were unanticipated but gave rise to some interesting analyses and directed our attention to the issue of tax complexity *per se*.

Our own view is that both simple and complex experiments may be appropriate. If you have a clear idea of your aims and those aims are straightforward, a simple experiment will be the most efficient. If you want to explore issues like tax loopholes and legal complexity you have no alternative but to use complex experiments.

Before coming to our final conclusions, it might be suitable to present a short recapitulation of our most important findings. The inequity variable, as brought forward in some of our experiments, did not influence subjects' fiscal behaviour. The role of equity might be restricted to that of a rationalisation on the part of respondents. Similarly, comparing subjects' earnings with each other did not lead to changes in evasion behaviour as well. This leaves the causal function of social comparison on evasion unclear.

Our two other experimentally manipulated factors, decision frame and opportunity to evade, showed more clear-cut results. Decision frames are linked to tax evasion in that receiving a refund in taxes from the revenue authorities, which is seen as a gain, reduces the inclination to evade. In contrast to this, an additional payment of taxes to the authorities, which is seen as a loss, increases the likelihood of evasion. Opportunity to cheat, defined as the detectability of evasion, more or less shows that increased detectability leads to less evasion.

After each experiment, we administered a questionnaire to our respondents, which contained items aimed at measuring key concepts of our theoretical model. The results of the subsequent correlation analyses were rather mixed. In the experiments comprising weaker manipulations, these analyses resembled those reported by Elffers, Weigel, and Hessing (1987) for documented behaviour. Looking at the experiments containing strong manipulations, these correlational patterns disappear to a large extent. These results suggest that strong situational pressures might suppress the effects of individual characteristics on tax-evasion behaviour, as emitted and measured in our simulation studies.

8.4 Conclusions

Many years ago, when we first began our experimental work on tax evasion, we believed it would be a quick and relatively easy way of obtaining useful data and untangling the causal structure of tax evasion. Experience has proved otherwise: it has turned out to be slow and difficult, though still, we would claim, useful. We do not wish here to reiterate our substantive findings; these are described in the concluding sections of chapters 3 and 4. But we will reflect a little on the approach and the future.

The least one can say is that anything helps in the difficult and awkward field of tax evasion – and the experimental approach is something. We would like to say a little more. If experiments are suitably designed they can make a substantial contribution to our understanding. Whether you are interested in the comprehensibility of tax forms, the role of socio-legal attitudes, compliance costs or deterrence, a good experiment will complement other sources of evidence. We now know quite a lot about what makes for a good experiment in this area (and perhaps even more about what makes for a bad one). It is crucial to minimise demand characteristics otherwise results may simply reflect participants' understanding of economics. We have achieved this by embedding the tax declarations in a small-business simulation, but this is only one possibility. It may be profitable in the future to devise a set-up that is more suitable for the individual taxpayer. This could involve, for example, a household budgeting task or a 'career' simulation in which participants made a wide variety of decisions relevant to their jobs and other aspects of their life. This might also facilitate the investigation of the process of tax evasion and enable us to explore the series of small decisions of which it is the result. Whether embedding is used or not, it is essential that the purpose of the experiment is not transparent. Another vital feature is that the operationalisations engage the same psychological processes as their counterparts in the everyday world. This may be extremely difficult for certain factors, as Long and Swingen remark, and despite cudgelling our brains for a few days we have not solved the problem they pose of operationalising stigma. For certain variables we may need in future to put our computers to one side or devise set-ups where the computer is only one aspect of the experimental situation.

On the negative side we have learnt that apparently small variations in procedures can have quite large effects. This suggests that great care must be taken with all aspects of running a tax experiment. To take just one example, we suspect that different kinds of recruitment subtly alter the nature of the implicit contract between the participant and the experiment and this may alter overall levels of evasion or, more seriously, interact with some manipulations. We have also grown wary of using student samples, though under certain conditions, for example when they are experienced taxpayers and prepared to take an experiment seriously, their use can be justified. Finally, we are very aware that the experimental situation as it stands is essentially individualistic. Tax evasion is a social phenomenon and shared beliefs about evasion and the membership of social groups matter. To incorporate the social aspects of evasion is a major challenge for the future.

The *Zeitgeist* in European social psychology is concentrated on rhetoric, discourse, and ideology, and qualitative methods are favoured. So it comes as no surprise that a reviewer of our most recent paper on tax evasion characterised our approach as old-fashioned. But traditional things have many virtues, not least of which is durability, and we believe that experimental approaches will outlast current fashions. We certainly hope so.

In these last chapters we have exposed our research to critical commentary in the belief that in this way lies progress. Some taxpayers may evade the scrutiny of the authorities and be secretive about their financial affairs: whatever the differences in our own personal beliefs about the legitimacy of tax evasion we are unanimous that scientific affairs should always be scrutinised.

References

Adams, J. S. (1965). Inequity in social exchange. *Advances in Experimental Social Psychology, 2,* 267–99

Adams, J. S., and Freedman, S. (1976). Equity theory revisited: Comments and annotated bibliography. *Advances in Experimental Social Psychology, 9,* 43–90

Aitken, S. S., and Bonneville, L. (1980). *A general taxpayer opinion survey.* IRS, Office of Planning and Research

Ajzen, I., and Fishbein, M. (1980). *Understanding attitudes and predicting behaviour.* Englewood Cliffs, NJ: Prentice-Hall

Allan, C. M. (1971). *The theory of taxation.* Harmondsworth: Penguin

Allingham, M. G., and Sandmo, A. (1972). Income tax evasion: A theoretical analysis. *Journal of Public Economics, 1,* 323–38

Alm, J. (1988). Compliance costs and the tax avoidance–tax evasion decision. *Public Finance Quarterly, 16,* 31–66

Alm, J., Bahl, S., and Murray, M. N. (1989). *Tax structure and tax compliance.* Unpublished manuscript, University of Tennessee

Alm, J., Jackson, B., and McKee, M. (1988). *The effects of uncertainty and ambiguity on taxpayer behavior.* Paper presented at the IRS Research Conference, Washington, DC (see IRS Document 7302 (6–89))

Alm, J., McClelland, G. M., and Schulze, W. D. (1989). *Why do people pay taxes?* Paper presented at the Law and Society Meeting, Madison, WI

Alvira Martin, F., and Garcia Lopez, J. (1984). *Taxation and income distribution.* Paper presented at the 9th Annual Colloquium of Economic Psychology, Tilburg, June

Anderson, G., and Brown, R. I. F. (1984). Real and laboratory gambling, sensation seeking and arousal: Towards a pavlovian component in general theories of gambling and gambling addiction. *British Journal of Psychology, 75,* 401–10

Antaki, C. (ed.) (1981). *The psychology of ordinary explanations of social behaviour.* London: Academic Press

Aronson, E., and Carlsmith, J. (1968). Experimentation in social psychology. In G. Lindzey and E. Aronson (eds.), *Handbook of Social Psychology,* vol. II (1–79). Reading, MA: Addison-Wesley

Baldry, J. C. (1986). Tax evasion is not a gamble: A report on two experiments. *Economics Letters, 22,* 333–5

(1987). Income tax evasion and the tax schedule: Some experimental results. *Public Finance, 42,* 357–83

Barr, N. A., James, S. R., and Prest, A. R. (1977). *Self-assessment for income tax.* London: Heinemann Educational Books

145

Baumeister, R. F. (1982). A self-presentational view of social phenomena. *Psychological Bulletin, 91*, 3–26

Beck, P. J., Davis, J. S., and Jung, W. O. (1989). *Economic determinants of taxpayer aggressiveness: Experimental evidence.* Paper presented at the annual meeting of the American Accounting Association, Honolulu

Becker, G. S. (1968). Crime and punishment: An economic approach. *Journal of Political Economy, 76*, 169–217

Becker, W., Büchner, H-J., and Sleeking, S. (1987). The impact of public expenditures on tax evasion: An experimental approach. *Journal of Public Economics, 34*, 243–52

Bell, C. G., and Buchanan, W. (1966). Reliable and unreliable respondents: Party registration and prestige pressure. *Western Political Quarterly, 19*, 37–43

Benjamini, Y., and Maital, S. (1985). Optimal tax evasion and optimal tax evasion policy: Behavioral aspects. In W. Gärtner and A. Wenig (eds.), *The economics of the shadow economy* (pp. 245–64). Berlin: Springer

Berghuis, A. C., and Kommer, M. M. (1984). *Opinies over belastingontduiking en uitkeringsmisbruik, en over maatregelen ter bestrijding daarvan* (Opinions about tax evasion and social-security fraud, and ways of controlling them). WODC-rapport 48. Staatsuitgeverij: 's-Gravenhage

Blalock, H. M. (1975). Indirect measurement in social science: Some nonadditive models. In H. M. Blalock, A. Aganbegian, F. Borodkin, R. Boudon, and V. Capecchi (eds.), *Quantitive Sociology: International perspectives on mathematical and statistical modeling* (pp. 359–79). New York: Academic Press

(1982). *Conceptualization and measurement in the social sciences.* Beverly Hills: Sage

Bracewell-Milnes, B. (1979). *Tax avoidance and evasion: The individual and society.* London: Panopticum Press

Broehm, K. A., and Sharp, K. (1989). *Summary of public attitude survey findings.* 1989 Update: Trend analyses and related statistics, IRS Document 6011 (6–89), 65–78

Broesterhuizen, G. A. A. M. (1985). The unobserved economy and the national accounts in the Netherlands. In W. Gärtner and A. Wenig (eds.), *The economics of the shadow economy* (pp. 105–26). Berlin: Springer

Brookshire, D. S., Coursey, D. L., and Schulze, W. D. (1987). The external validity of experimental economics techniques: Analysis of demand behavior. *Economic Inquiry, 25*, 239–50

Brown, C. V., Levin, E. J., Rosa, P. J., and Ulph, D. T. (1984). Tax evasion and avoidance on earned income: Some survey evidence. *Fiscal Studies, 5(3)*, 1–22

Calahan, D. (1968). Correlates of respondent accuracy in the Denver reliability survey. *Public Opinion Quarterly, 32*, 608–21

Carroll, J. S. (1987). Compliance with the law: A decision-making approach to taxpaying. *Law and Human Behavior, 11*, 319–35

(1989). A cognitive-process approach of taxpayer compliance. In J. A. Roth and J. T. Scholz (eds.), *Taxpayer compliance: Volume 2. Social science perspectives* (pp. 228–72). Philadelphia: University of Pennsylvania Press

Casey, J. T., and Scholz, J. T. (in press). Boundary effects of vague risk information on taxpayer decisions. *Organizational Behavior and Human Decision Processes*

Chang, O. H., Nichols, D. R., and Schultz, J. J. (1987). Taxpayer attitudes towards tax audit risk. *Journal of Economic Psychology, 8,* 299–309

Cialdini, R. B. (1989). Social motivations to comply: Norms, values, and principles. In J. A. Roth and J. T. Scholz (eds.), *Taxpayer compliance: Volume 2. Social science perspectives* (pp. 200–27). Philadelphia: University of Pennsylvania Press

Clotfelter, C. T. (1983). Tax evasion and tax rates: An analysis of individual returns. *Review of Economics and Statistics, 65,* 363–73

Contini, B. (1981). Labor market segmentation and the development of the parallel economy – the Italian experience. *Oxford Economic Papers, 33,* 401–12

Corchon, L. (1984). A note on tax evasion and the theory of games. Mimeo, Madrid

Cowell, F. A. (1985). The economic analysis of tax evasion. *Bulletin of Economic Research, 37,* 163–93

(1990). *Cheating the government.* Cambridge, MA: MIT Press

Cox, D., and Plumley, A. (1988). *Analyses of voluntary compliance rates for different income source classes.* Unpublished report. International Revenue Service, Research Division: Washington, DC

Cross, R., and Shaw, G. K. (1982). On the economics of tax aversion. *Public Finance, 37,* 36–47

Cullis, J., and Lewis, A. (1985). Some hypotheses and evidence on tax knowledge and preferences. *Journal of Economic Psychology, 6,* 271–87

Cyert, R. M., and March, J. G. (1963). *A behavioral theory of the firm.* Englewood Cliffs, NJ: Prentice-Hall

Dawes, R. M. (1980). Social dilemmas. *Annual Review of Psychology, 31,* 169–93

DeJong, D. V., Forsythe, R., and Uecker, W. C. (1988). A note on the use of businessmen in sealed offer markets. *Journal of Economic Behavior and Organization, 9,* 87–100

De Juan, A. (1989). *Fiscal attitudes and behavior: A study of 16–35 year old Swedish citizens.* The EFI Research Report 285. Stockholm: Stockholm School of Economics

Doise, W. (1986). *Levels of explanation in social psychology.* Cambridge: Cambridge University Press

Dornstein, M. (1976). Compliance with legal and bureaucratic rules: The case of self-employed taxpayers in Israel. *Human Relations, 29,* 1019–34.

Drost, T. R., and Jongman, R. W. (1982). Ontduiking van inkomstenbelasting. In A. J. Hoekama and J. Van Houtte (eds.), *De rechtssociologische werkkamer* (In the study of sociology of law) (pp. 133–54). Deventer: Van Loghum Slaterus

Dubin, J. A., and Wilde, L. L. (1988). An empirical analysis of federal income tax auditing and compliance. *National Tax Journal, 41,* 61–74

Eiser, J. R. (1986). *Social psychology: Attitudes, cognition and behavior.* Cambridge: Cambridge University Press

Elffers, H., Hessing, D. J., and Robben, H. S. J. (1989). *De aanslagregeling inkomstenbelasting bij particulieren: Werkwijze en effectiviteit* (The auditing process of non-business income-tax returns: Method and efficacy). Rotterdam: Erasmus University

Elffers, H., Robben, H. S. J., and Hessing, D. J. (1991). Under-reporting income. Who is the best judge – taxpayer or tax inspector? *Journal of the Royal Statistical Society* (Series A, 154, part 1), 125–7

Elffers, H., Weigel, R. H., and Hessing, D. J. (1987). The consequences of different strategies for measuring tax evasion behavior. *Journal of Economic Psychology, 8,* 311-37

Erekson, O. H., and Sullivan, D. H. (1988). A cross-section analysis of IRS auditing. *National Tax Journal, 41,* 175-89.

Etzioni, A. (1986). Tax evasion and perceptions of tax fairness: A research note. *Journal of Applied Behavioral Science, 22,* 177-85

Feige, E. L. (1979). How big is the irregular economy? *Challenge, Nov.-Dec.,* 5-13

Festinger, L. (1954). A theory of social comparison processes. *Human Relations, 7,* 117-40

Fincham, F. D., and Jaspars, J. M. F. (1980). Attribution of responsibility: From man the scientist to man the lawyer. *Advances in Experimental Social Psychology, 13,* 82-138

Fishbein, M., and Ajzen, I. (1974). Attitudes towards objects as predictors of single and multiple behavioral criteria. *Psychological Reviews, 81,* 59-74

  (1975). *Belief, attitude, intention and behavior: An introduction to theory and research.* Reading, MA: Addison-Wesley

Freedman, J. L. (1969). Role playing: Psychology by consensus. *Journal of Personality and Social Psychology, 13,* 107-14

Frey, B. S., and Weck, H. (1987). Estimating the shadow economy: A 'naive' approach. *Oxford Economic Papers, 35,* 23-44

Friedland, N. (1982). A note on tax evasion as a function of the quality of information about the magnitude and credibility of threatened fines: Some preliminary research. *Journal of Applied Social Psychology, 12,* 54-9

Friedland, N., Maital, S., and Rutenberg, A. (1978). A simulation study of income tax evasion. *Journal of Public Economics, 10,* 107-16

Goode, R. (1976). *The individual income tax.* Washington DC: The Brookings Institute

Grasmick, H. G., and Scott, W. J. (1982). Tax evasion and mechanisms of social control: A comparison with grand and petty theft. *Journal of Economic Psychology, 2,* 213-30

Greenberg, J. (1984). Avoiding tax avoidance: A (repeated) game theoretic approach. *Journal of Economic Theory, 32,* 1-13

Groenland, E. A. G., and Van Veldhoven, G. M. (1983). Tax evasion behavior: A psychological framework. *Journal of Economic Psychology, 3,* 129-44

Groenland, E. A. G., and Van Zon, I. (1984). *Tax evasion behavior: An empirical exploration.* Paper presented at the 9th Annual Colloquium of Economic Psychology, Tilburg, June

Güth, W., and Mackscheidt, K. (1985). An empirical study of tax evasion. Mimeo, University of Cologne

Guttman, P. M. (1977). The subterranean economy. *Financial Analysts Journal, Nov.-Dec.,* 26-8

Guze, S. B., and Goodwin, D. W. (1972). Consistency of drinking history and diagnosis of alcoholism. *Quarterly Journal of Studies on Alcohol, 33,* 111-16

Hagemann, R. P., Jones, B. R., and Montador, R. B. (1988). Tax reform in OECD countries: Motives, constraints and practice. *OECD Economic Studies, 10,* 185-226

Hardin, G. (1968). The tragedy of the commons. *Science, 162,* 1243-8

Hauber, A. R., Toornvliet, L. G., and Willemse, H. M. (1986). Persoonlijkheid en criminaliteit (Personality and crime). *Tijdschrift voor Criminologie, 2*, 92–106

Haycraft, J. (1985). *Italian labyrinth.* Harmondsworth: Penguin

Heider, F. (1958). *The psychology of interpersonal relations.* New York: John Wiley and Sons

Henry, S. (1978). *The hidden economy.* London: Martin Robertson

Hessing, D. J., and Elffers, H. (1985). Economic man or social man? In H. Brandstätter and E. Kirchler (eds.), *Economic psychology* (pp. 195–203). Linz: Trauner

Hessing, D. J., Elffers, H., and Robben, H. S. J. (1987). The invalidity of self-reported tax evasion: Further evidence based on triangulation of measurement strategies. In F. Ölander (ed.), *Understanding economic behaviour* (pp. 149–64). Århus: Handelshøjskolen

Hessing, D. J., Elffers, H., and Weigel, R. H. (1988). Exploring the limits of self-reports and reasoned action: An investigation of the psychology of tax evasion behavior. *Journal of Personality and Social Psychology, 54*, 405–13

Hessing, D. J., Kinsey, K. A., Elffers, H., and Weigel, R. H. (1988). Tax evasion research: Measurement strategies and theoretical models. In W. F. Van Raaij, G. M. van Veldhoven, and K.-E. Wärneryd (eds.), *Handbook of economic psychology* (pp. 516–37). Dordrecht: Kluwer

Hessing, D. J., Robben, H. S. J., and Elffers, H. (1989). *The relationship between self-reported and documented behavior in the case of fraud with unemployment benefits.* Paper presented at the 1989 Annual Meeting of the Law and Society Association, Madison, WI

Hite, P. A. (1987). An application of attribution theory in taxpayer noncompliance research. *Public Finance, 42*, 105–18

Hite, P. A., Jackson, B. R., and Spicer, M. W. (1988). The effect of framing biases on taxpayer compliance. Unpublished manuscript

Hood, R., and Sparks, R. (1970). *Key issues in Criminology.* New York: McGraw-Hill

Internal Revenue Service (1988a). *Income tax compliance research: Gross tax gap estimates and projections for 1973–1992.* Publication 7285 (March 1988), Research Division

(1988b). *Change and complexity as barriers to taxpayer compliance.* Proceedings of the IRS Research Conference (Document 7302 (6–89))

(1989). *1988 Annual report of the Commissioner and Chief Counsel of the Internal Revenue Service.* Washington, DC: US Government Printing Office

Isachsen, A. J., Samuelson, S. O., and Strøm, S. (1985). The behavior of tax evaders. In W. Gärtner and A. Wenig (eds.), *The economics of the shadow economy* (pp. 227–44). Berlin: Springer

Jackson, B., and Jones, S. (1985). Salience of tax evasion penalties versus detection risk. *Journal of the American Taxation Association, Spring*, 7–17

Jackson, B. R., and Milliron, V. C. (1986). Tax compliance research: Findings, problems, and prospects. *Journal of Accounting Literature, 5*, 125–65

James, S. R., Lewis, A., and Allison, F. (1987). *The comprehensibility of taxation.* London: Gower

Jaspars, J. M. F., Hewstone, M., and Fincham, F. D. (1983). Attribution theory and research: The state of the art. In J. M. F. Jaspars, F. D. Fincham, and M. Hewstone (eds.), *Attribution theory and research: Conceptual, developmental and social dimensions* (pp. 3–36). London: Academic Press

Jessor, R., Graves, T. D., Hansen, R. C., and Jessor, S. L. (1968). *Society, personality and deviant behavior: A study of a tri-ethnic community.* New York: Holt, Rhinehart, and Winston

Johnson, D. W., and Norem-Hebeisen, A. A. (1979). A measure of cooperative, competitive and individualistic attitudes. *Journal of Social Psychology, 109,* 253–61

Jones, E. E., and Davis, K. E. (1965). From acts to dispositions. *Advances in Experimental Social Psychology, 3,* 1–24

Jung, J. (1982). *The experimenter's challenge.* London: Collier Macmillan

Kagan, R. A. (1989). On the visibility of income tax law violations. In J. A. Roth and J. T. Scholz (eds.), *Taxpayer compliance: Volume 2. Social science perspectives* (pp. 76–125). Philadelphia: University of Pennsylvania Press

Kahneman, D., and Tversky, A. (1979). Prospect theory: An analysis of decision under risk. *Econometrica, 47,* 263–91

Tversky, A. (1984). Choices, values and frames. *American Psychologist, 39,* 341–50

Kaplan, S. E., Reckers, P. M. J., and Reynolds, K. D. (1986). An application of attribution and equity theories to tax evasion behavior. *Journal of Economic Psychology, 7,* 461–6

Keith, Lord of Kinkel PC, chairman (1983). *Report of the Committee on Enforcement Powers of the Revenue Departments, Volumes I and II.* London: Her Majesty's Stationery Office

Kelley, H. H. (1967). Attribution theory in social psychology. *Nebraska symposium on Motivation, 15,* 192–238

Kelman, H. C. (1965). Manipulation of human behavior: An ethical dilemma for the social scientist. *Journal of Social Issues, 21,* 31–46

Kinsey, K. A. (1984). *Theories and models of tax cheating.* Taxpayer Compliance Project Working Paper 84-2: Chicago, IL: American Bar Foundation

(1986). Theories and models of tax cheating. *Criminal Justice Abstracts, 18,* 403–25

(1988). *Measurement bias or honest disagreement? Problems of validating measures of tax evasion.* ABF Working Paper no. 8811. Chicago, Il: American Bar Foundation

Klepper, S., and Nagin, D. (1989). Tax compliance and perceptions of the risks of detection and criminal prosecution. *Law and Society Review, 23,* 209–40

Kristiansen, C. M. (1985). Values related to preventive health behaviour. *Journal of Personality and Social Psychology, 49,* 748–58

Laurin, U. (1986). *På heder och samvete: Skattefuskets orsaker och utbredning* (Upon my honour: The causes and extent of tax evasion). Stockholm: Norstedts

Lawler, E. E. (1968). Effects of hourly overpayment on productivity and work quality. *Journal of Personality and Social Psychology, 10,* 306–13

Lea, S. E. G., Tarpy, R. M., and Webley, P. (1987). *The individual in the economy.* Cambridge: Cambridge University Press

Lewis, A. (1982). *The psychology of taxation.* Oxford: Martin Robertson

Lewis, A., and Cullis, J. (1988). Preferences, economics and the economic psychology of public sector preference formation. *Journal of Behavioral Economics, 17,* 19–33

Liebrand, W. B. G. (1982). Interpersonal differences in social dilemmas: A game theoretic approach. Unpublished doctoral dissertation, State University of Groningen

(1984). The effects of social motives, communication and group size on behavior in an n-person multi-stage mixed-motive game. *European Journal of Social Psychology, 14, 239–64*

Loftus, E. F. (1985). To file, perchance to cheat. *Psychology Today, April, 35–9*

Long, S. B. (1980). *The Internal Revenue Service: Measuring tax offenses and enforcement response.* Washington, DC: US Government Printing Office

(1981). Social control in the civil law: The case of income tax enforcement. In H. L. Ross (ed.), *Law and deviance* (pp. 185–214). Beverly Hills: Sage

(1989). *The impact of the Tax Reform Act of 1986 on compliance burdens: Preliminary national survey results.* Paper presented at the 1989 IRS Research Conference

Long, S. B., and Schwartz, R. D. (1987). *The impact of IRS audits on taxpayer compliance: A field experiment in specific deterrence.* Paper presented at the annual meeting of the Law and Society Association, Madison, WI

Long, S. B., and Swingen, J. A. (1988). The role of legal complexity in shaping taxpayer compliance. In P. J. Van Koppen, D. J. Hessing, and G. Van den Heuvel (eds.), *Lawyers on psychology and psychologists on law* (pp. 127–46). Amsterdam: Swets and Zeitlinger

(1989). The success of law in mandating duties. *Proceedings of the 82nd annual meeting of the National Tax Association/Tax Institute of America.* Columbus, OH: National Tax Association

McCrohan, K. F. (1982). The use of survey research to estimate trends in non-compliance with federal incomes taxes. *Journal of Economic Psychology, 2, 231–40*

McKee, T. C., and Gerbing, M. D. (1989). *Taxpayer perceptions of fairness: The TRA of 1986.* Paper presented at the 1989 IRS Research Conference, Washington, DC. (See IRS Document 7302, forthcoming)

Maital, S. (1982). *Minds, markets and money.* New York: Basic Books

March, J. G., and Simon, H. A. (1958). *Organizations.* New York: John Wiley and Sons

Masling, J. (1966). Role-related behavior of the subject and psychologist and its effects upon psychological data. *Nebraska Symposium on Motivation, 14, 67–103*

Mason, R., and Calvin, L. D. (1978). A study of admitted tax evasion. *Law and Society Review, 13, 73–89*

Mason, R., and Lowry, H. M. (1981). *An estimate of income tax evasion in Oregon.* Oregon State University, Corvallis, Survey Research Center

Medanik, L. (1982). The validity of self-reported alcohol consumption and alcohol problems: A literature review. *British Journal of Addiction, 77, 357–82*

Messere, K. C., and Owens, J. P. (1987). International comparisons of tax levels: Pitfalls and insights. *OECD Economic Studies, 8, 93–119*

Milgram, S. (1974). *Obedience to authority.* London: Tavistock

Montgomery, H., Drottz, B.-M., Gärling, T., Persson, A.-L., and Waara, R. (1985). Conceptions about material and immaterial values in a sample of Swedish subjects. In H. Brandstätter and E. Kirchler (eds.), *Economic psychology* (pp. 427–37). Linz: Trauner

Neal, A. G., and Rettig, S. (1967). On the multi-dimensionality of alienation. *American Sociological Review, 32, 54–64*

Oort Commission (1986). *A step towards simplicity.* The Hague: Ministry of Finance, The Netherlands

Orne, M. T. (1962). On the social psychology of the psychological experiment. *American Psychologist*, 17, 776–83

Phillips, D. L. (1971). *Knowledge from what? Theories and methods in social research.* Chicago: Rand McNally

Platt, C. J. (1980). *Tax systems in Western Europe.* Farnborough: Gower

(1982). *Tax systems of Africa, Asia and the Middle East.* Farnborough: Gower

Potter, J., and Wetherall, M. (1987). *Discourse and social psychology: Beyond attitudes and behaviour.* London: Sage

Raj, S. P. (1982). The effects of advertising on high and low loyalty consumer segments. *Journal of Consumer Research*, 9, 77–89

Rijsman, J. B. (1974). Factors in social comparison of performance influencing actual performance. *European Journal of Social Psychology*, 4, 279–311

(1983). The dynamics of social competition in personal and social comparison situations. In W. Doise and S. Moscovici (eds.), *Current issues in European social psychology* (pp. 279–312). Cambridge: Cambridge University Press

Robben, H. S. J., Elffers, H., and Verlind, W. F. M. (1989). *Determinanten van individueel misbruik van sociale verzekeringen: Het geval van WW-misbruik* (Determinants of individual abuse of social security: The case of fraud with unemployment benefits). Amsterdam: Federatie van Bedrijfsverenigingen

Robben, H. S. J., Hessing, D. J., and Elffers, H. (1990). Legal controls and type of employment in tax evasion behavior. In S. E. G. Lea, P. Webley, and B. M. Young (eds.), *Applied economic psychology in the 1990s* (pp. 512–22). Exeter: Washington Singer Press

Robben, H. S. J., Webley, P., Weigel, R. H., Wärneryd, K-E., Kinsey, K. A., Hessing D. J., Alvira Martin, F., Elffers, H., Wahlund, R., Van Langenhove, L., Long, S. B., and Scholz, J. T. (1990). Decision frame and opportunity as determinants of tax cheating: An international experimental study. *Journal of Economic Psychology*, 11, 341–64

Robins, L. N. (1963). The reluctant respondent. *Public Opinion Quarterly*, 27, 276–86

Rokeach, M. (1973). *The nature of human values.* New York: The Free Press

Rose, R., and Karran, T. (1987). *Taxation by political inertia.* London: Allen and Unwin

Roth, A. E. (1986). Laboratory experimentation in economics. *Economics and Philosophy*, 2, 245–73

Roth, A. E. (ed.) (1987). *Laboratory experimentation in economics: Six points of view.* Cambridge: Cambridge University Press

Royal Commission on Taxation (1966). Ottawa: Queen's Printer and Controller of Stationery

Rundquist, E. A., and Sletto, R. F. (1936). *Personality in the depression.* Minneapolis: University of Minnesota Press

Sabine, B. E. V. (1966). *A history of income tax.* London: Allen and Unwin

Sandford, C. T. (1973). *Hidden costs of taxation.* London: Institute for Fiscal Studies

Sandford, C. T., Godwin, M., Hardwick, P., and Butterworth, I. (1981). *Costs and benefits of VAT.* London: Heinemann Educational Books

Schadewald, M. S. (1989). Reference point effects in taxpayer decision making. *Journal of the American Taxation Association, Spring*, 68–84

Schmölders, G. (1959). Fiscal psychology: A new branch of public finance. *National Tax Journal*, 12, 340–5

(1970). Survey research in public finance: A behavioral approach to fiscal theory. *Public Finance*, 25, 300–6

Scholz, J. T. (1985). Coping with complexity: A bounded rationality perspective on taxpayer compliance. *Proceedings of the 78th annual conference of the National Tax Association/Tax Institute of America.* Columbus, OH: National Tax Association

Schwartz, R. D., and Orleans, S. (1967). On legal sanctions. *University of Chicago Law Review, 34,* 282–300

Scott, W. J., and Grasmick, H. G. (1981). Deterrence and income tax cheating: Testing interaction hypotheses in utilitarian theories. *Journal of Applied Behavioral Science, 17,* 395–408

Silverman, I. (1977). Why social psychology fails. *Canadian Psychological Review, 18,* 353–8

Slemrod, J. (1985). An empirical test for tax evasion. *Review of Economics and Statistics, 5,* 232–8

Slemrod, J., and Sorum, N. (1984). The compliance cost of the US individual income tax system. *National Tax Journal, 37,* 461–74

Smith, K. W., and Kinsey, K. A. (1987). Understanding taxpaying behavior: A conceptual framework with implications for research. *Law and Society Review, 21,* 639–63

Smith, R., and Hunt, S. D. (1978). Attributional processes and effects in promotional situations. *Journal of Consumer Research, 5,* 149–58

Smith, S. (1986). *Britain's shadow economy.* Oxford: Oxford University Press

Smith, V. L. (1987). Experimental methods in economics. In J. Eatwell, M. Milgate, and P. Newman (eds.), *The New Palgrave: A dictionary of economic theory and doctrine* (pp. 241–9). London: Macmillan

Sobell, L. C. (1976). *The validity of self-reports; Toward a predictive model.* Ph.D. dissertation: University of California, Irvine, Ann Arbor, Michigan: Xerox University Microfilms

Spicer, M. W., and Becker, L. A. (1980). Fiscal inequity and tax evasion: An experimental approach. *National Tax Journal, 33,* 172–5

Spicer, M. W., and Hero, R. E. (1985). Tax evasion and heuristics: A research note. *Journal of Public Economics, 26,* 263–7

Spicer, M. W., and Lundstedt, S. B. (1976). Understanding tax evasion. *Public Finance, 31,* 295–305

Spicer, M. W., and Thomas, J. E. (1982). Audit probabilities and the tax evasion decision: An experimental approach. *Journal of Economic Psychology, 2,* 241–5

Srole, L. (1956). Social integration and certain corollaries. *American Sociological Review, 21,* 709–16

Stalans, L. J., Smith, K. W., and Kinsey, K. A. (1989). When do we think about detection? Structural opportunity and taxpaying behavior. *Law and Social Inquiry, 14,* 481–503

Stephens, R. (1972). The truthfulness of addict responses in research projects. *International Journal of Addictions, 7,* 549–58

Sudman, S., and Bradburn, N. M. (1974). *Response effects in surveys: A review and synthesis.* Chicago: Aldine

Swingen, J. A. (1989). *Taxpayer attitudes and equity perceptions after the Tax Reform Act of 1986.* Paper presented at the 1989 IRS Research Conference, Washington, DC. (See IRS Document 7302, forthcoming)

Swingen, J. A., and Long, S. B. (1988a). A look back at the 1988 filing season. *Tax Notes, December 19,* 1343–7

(1988b). Mathematical and clerical errors during the 1987 filing season. *Tax Notes, May 9,* 759–65

154   *References*

Tajfel, H., and Fraser, C. (1978). *Introducing social psychology*. Harmondsworth: Penguin.

Tanzi, V. (1980). Inflation and the personal income tax: An international perspective. Cited in Maital (1982)

Tedeschi, J. T., and Reiss, M. (1981). Predicaments and verbal tactics of impression management. In C. Antaki (ed.), *Ordinary language explanation of social behaviour*. London: Academic Press

Tetlock, P. E., and Manstead, A. S. R. (1985). Impression management versus intra-psychic explanations in social psychology: A useful dichotomy? *Psychological Review*, *92*, 59–77

Tversky, A., and Kahneman, D. (1981). The framing of decisions and the psychology of choice. *Science*, *211*, 453–8

US Bureau of Census (1987). *Statistical abstract of the United States (107th edition)*. Washington DC

Van Bijsterveld, W. J. (1980). *Aangepaste versie van het verslag van een onderzoek naar de aard en omvang van de belastingfraude* (Adapted version of the report on an investigation into the nature and extent of tax fraud). 's-Gravenhage: Staatsdrukkerij

Van der Pligt, J. (1986). Probleembeschrijving en voorkeur voor zekere versus onzekere alternatieven (Problem description and preference for certain versus uncertain alternatives). In A. Van Knippenberg, M. Poppe, J. Extra, G. J. Kok, and E. Seydel (eds.), *Fundamentele sociale psychologie* (pp. 170–91). Tilburg: Tilburg University Press

Van der Pligt, J., and Eiser, J. R. (1984). Dimensional salience, judgement and attitudes. In J. R. Eiser (ed.), *Attitudinal judgement* (pp. 161–78). New York: Springer

Van Eck, R., and Kazemier, B. (1985). Zwarte inkomsten uit arbeid: Resultaten van in 1983 gehouden experimentele enquetes (Earning income on the side: Results of experimental questionnaires administered in 1983). *Statistische Katernen No. 3*. Voorburg: Centraal Bureau Voor de Statistiek

(1988). Features of the hidden economy in the Netherlands. *The Review of Income and Wealth*, *34*, 251–73

Van Raaij, W. F. (1985). Attribution of causality to economic actions and events. *Kyklos*, *38*, 3–19

Vogel, J. (1974). Taxation and public opinion in Sweden: An interpretation of recent survey data. *National Tax Journal*, *27*, 499–513

Wallschutzky, I. G. (1984). Possible causes of tax evasion. *Journal of Economic Psychology*, *5*, 371–84

Walsh, D., and Poole, A. (1983). *A dictionary of criminology*. London: Routledge and Kegan Paul

Wärneryd, K.-E. (1980). Psychological reactions to the tax system. *Skandinaviska Enskilda Banken Quarterly Review*, *3–4*, 75–84.

Wärneryd, K.-E., and Walerud, B. (1982). Taxes and economic behavior: Some interview data on tax evasion in Sweden. *Journal of Economic Psychology*, *2*, 187–211

Watson, D. (1982). The actor and the observer: How are their perceptions of causality divergent? *Psychological Bulletin*, *92*, 682–700

Weaver, F. M., and Carroll, J. S. (1985). Crime perceptions in a natural setting by expert and novice shoplifters. *Social Psychology Quarterly*, *48*, 349–59

Webb, E. J., Campbell, D. T., Schwartz, R. D., and Sechrest, L. (1966). *Unobtrusive measures: Nonreactive research in the social sciences.* New York: Rand McNally

Webley, P. (1987). Audit probabilities and tax evasion in a business simulation. *Economics Letters, 25,* 267–70

Webley, P., and Halstead, S. (1986). Tax evasion on the micro: Significant simulations or expedient experiments? *Journal of Interdisciplinary Economics, 1,* 87–100

Weigel, R. H., Hessing, D. J., and Elffers, H. (1987). Tax evasion research: A critical appraisal and a theoretical model. *Journal of Economic Psychology, 8,* 215–35

Winer, B. J. (1971). *Statistical principles in experimental design* (2nd edition). New York: McGraw-Hill

Witte, A. D., and Woodbury, D. F. (1985). The effect of tax laws and tax administration on tax compliance: The case of the US individual income tax. *National Tax Journal, 38,* 1–13

Wolfe, A. C. (1974). *1973 US national breathtaking survey.* HIT Laboratory Reports, University of Michigan, 4, 1–15

Wright, J. (1819). *Parliamentary history,* vol. XXXIV, 1798–1800. London: T. C. Hansard

Zeller, R. A., Neal, A. G., and Groat, H. T. (1980). On the reliability and stability of alienation measures: A longitudinal analysis. *Social Forces, 58,* 1195–204

Zuckerman, M. (1979). *Dimensions of sensation seeking: Beyond the optimal level of arousal.* Hillsdale, NJ: Erlbaum

Subject index

attitudes 14, 22
attribution theory 18–19
audit probability 9, 86, 87, 88, 90
awareness of behaviour 34

behavioural
    decision theory 81
    outcome measure 21
    simulation measure 21

celerity 16
collection costs 6
combined data 36–9
complexity 138, 142
compliance costs 15, 28
conscience, appeals to 7
constraints 20
controls
    legal 21, 22
    social 21, 22
cross-national comparison 75, 78

decision 11
    content 16
    frame 102, 104, 107, 108, 113, 142
    process 16
deductions
    itemisation of 9
    overstating 5
demand characteristics 45, 46, 143
demographic characteristics 22, 58
detection
    fear of 8
    probability of 8, 9, 10
deterrence process 5, 6
dissatisfaction 23
documented behaviour 22, 23, 35

economic models 8–13, 126
equilibrium 10, 11
equity 55, 56, 60, 62, 63, 68, 69, 78, 142
estimates 3
    direct 3, 29–33
    indirect 3, 4, 29, 33–9

exchange relationship 17, 55
expected rate of return 125, 139, 140
experimental
    approach 39–44
    design 129

financial strain 20, 21 92
fiscal connection 16
framing 12, 79, 82, 135

guilt 18

habitual
    behaviour 16
    response 16
hidden labour 6

identification 18
impression management 34
income, underreporting 5, 6
individual differences, 9, 17, 20, 58–60, 86, 90, 108, 109, 110, 143
inertia 15, 80
instigations 20
integrative models 13
interactive models 10
internalisation 18
intolerance 21
involvement 115, 121

multiple measurement 53

norms 22
    acquisition 16

official records 3, 31
opportunity 5, 14, 15, 17, 20, 21, 22, 35, 85, 86, 87, 89, 90, 102, 105, 106, 107, 108, 112, 113, 142
    perceived 21, 22

Pay As You Earn 24, 26, 27
penalties 8, 9, 136, 137
perceived risk of punishment 21
perceptions 14

personal
  orientation 20, 21
  strain 20, 21
personality traits 14
policy 7, 14, 123
prospect theory 11, 12, 16, 82, 84, 92,
    102, 112
punishment, fear of 22

qualitative data 117

rationality
  bounded 81
  limited 10, 11
realism
  experimental 45, 114, 115
  mundane 45, 115
real-life behaviour 118, 119
reputation 8
returns, not filing 6

salience 80
sampling 47
sanctions 7, 10
self-employed 5, 9, 20, 28, 35, 85
self-presentational concerns 112
self-reports 3, 21, 22, 23, 32, 33, 34,
    35, 37, 112
shadow economy 30
simultaneous equations 53
situational characteristics 17
small-business simulation 46, 48, 143
social
  comparison 55, 57, 60, 63, 69, 70,
    72, 76, 77, 78, 142
  context 15, 16
  dilemma 19, 20, 22, 23
  norms 20, 21

orientation 17
social psychological models 13–23
social-security fraud 23
socio-economic factors 17

tax
  avoidance 2, 128, 135
  bands 27
  cheating 3
  compliance 2, 18
  definition 24
  direct 25
  enforcement 14, 28
  evasion 1, 2, 3, 7, 29, 128, 135, 136
  indirect 25
  mentality 23, 24, 28
  noncompliance 2, 3, 4, 5, 128, 136
  rate 8, 25
  resistance 1
  system 17, 23, 26, 28, 123
tax rates, marginal 25, 26
tax reform 7, 27
  act 1, 27
taxation 25
Taxpayer Compliance Measurement
    Program 3
taxpayer typology 17
triangulation 53

underground economy 4, 5
utility 8, 11, 12

validity 126, 140
  external 44, 129, 135, 139
values 86, 88, 89
voluntary compliance rate 83

withholding 84, 112

Author index

Adams, J. S., 55
Aitkin, S. S., 85
Ajzen, I., 14, 15, 16, 35, 38, 86
Allan, C. M., 25
Allingham, M. G., 8, 9, 81
Allison, F., 3, 15
Alm, J., 10, 130, 135
Alvira Martin, F., 24
Anderson, G., 45
Antaki, C., 19
Aronson, E., 45

Bahl, S., 135
Baldry, J. C., 32, 33, 39, 42, 43, 45, 46, 52, 82, 111
Barr, N. A., 6, 27
Baumeister, R. F., 34
Beck, P. J., 130
Becker, G. S., 8, 81
Becker, L. A., 40, 56, 62, 77
Becker, W., 42, 43
Bell, C. G., 34
Benjamini, Y., 10, 11, 57
Berghuis, A. C., 141
Blalock, H. M., 29, 53
Bonneville, L., 85
Bracewell-Milnes, B., 2
Bradburn, N. M., 34
Broehm, K. A., 1
Broesterhuizen, G. A. A. M., 4
Brookshire, D. S., 44
Brown, C. V., 6
Brown, R. I. F., 45
Buchanan, W., 34
Büchner, H.-J., 42, 43
Butterworth, I., 15

Calahan, D., 34
Calvin, L. D., 8, 56, 58, 68, 85
Campbell, D. T., 53
Carlsmith, J., 45
Carroll, J. S., 11, 29, 80, 81, 82, 84
Casey, J. T., 82
Chang, O. H., 82
Cialdini, R. B., 86

Clotfelter, C. T., 31, 59, 85, 113
Contini, B., 30
Corchon, L., 10
Coursey, D. L., 44
Cowell, F. A., 4, 8, 10, 11, 123, 139, 141, 142
Cox, D., 83
Cross, R., 135
Cullis, J., 14
Cyert, R. M., 81

Davis, J. S., 130
Davis, K. E., 18
Dawes, R. M., 44
DeJong, D. V., 44, 47, 102
De Juan, A., 56, 59, 62, 68, 85
Doise, W., 44
Dornstein, M., 58
Drost, T. R., 31, 37
Drottz, B.-M., 89
Dubin, J. A., 9, 113

Eiser, J. R., 15, 54
Elffers, H., 5, 6, 13, 17, 19, 21, 22, 23, 32, 34, 35, 36, 37, 38, 39, 54, 56, 58, 59, 60, 68, 69, 71, 73, 75, 76, 77, 79, 80, 82, 92, 109, 111, 112, 113, 123, 131, 137, 143
Erekson, O. H., 4
Etzioni, A., 1, 56

Feige, E. L., 4, 30
Festinger, L., 57
Fraser, C., 40
Frey, B. S., 30, 31, 75
Fincham, F. D., 19
Fishbein, M., 14, 15, 16, 35, 38, 86
Forsythe, R., 44, 47, 102
Freedman, J. L., 117
Freedman, S., 55
Friedland, N., 9, 39, 40, 41, 42, 48, 50, 51, 58

Garcia Lopez, J., 24
Gärling, T., 89

158

Gerbing, M. D., 1, 136
Godwin, M., 15
Goode, R., 1
Grasmick, H. G., 8, 33, 56
Graves, T. D., 19
Greenberg, J., 10
Groat, H. T., 73
Groenland, E. A. G., 5, 13, 17, 58, 59, 85
Güth, W., 42
Guttman, P. M., 4
Guze, S. B., 34

Hagemann, R. P., 7, 26
Halstead, S., 9, 41, 43, 47, 50, 52, 55, 78, 111, 114, 126
Hansen, R. C., 19
Hardin, G., 20
Hardwick, P., 15
Hauber, A. R., 73
Haycraft, J., 24
Heider, F., 18
Henry, S., 89
Hero, R. E., 40, 52, 77
Hessing, D. J., 5, 6, 13, 17, 19, 21, 22, 32, 34, 35, 36, 37, 38, 39, 54, 56, 58, 59, 60, 68, 69, 71, 73, 75, 76, 77, 79, 80, 82, 92, 109, 111, 112, 113, 123, 131, 137, 143
Hewstone, M., 19
Hite, P. A., 18, 19, 83
Hood, R., 34
Hunt, S. D., 18

Internal Revenue Service, 1, 27, 136
Isachsen, A. J., 141

Jackson, B. R., 9, 10, 12, 57, 58, 59, 83, 130
James, S. R., 3, 6, 15, 27
Jaspars, J. M., 19
Jessor, R., 19
Jessor, S. L., 19
Johnson, D. W., 20
Jones, B. R., 7, 26
Jones, E. E., 18
Jones, S., 9
Jongman, R. W., 31, 37
Jung, J., 47
Jung, W. O., 130

Kagan, R. A., 103
Kahneman, D., 10, 11, 12, 46, 54, 79, 82, 140
Kaplan, S. E., 13, 18, 19
Karran, T., 23
Kazemier, B., 4, 6, 9, 58
Keith, Lord of Kinkel PC, 135
Kelley, H. H., 18

Kelman, H. C., 17
Kinsey, K. A., 3, 4, 5, 6, 8, 10, 12, 13, 15, 17, 29, 35, 38, 39, 47, 53, 78, 80, 81, 82, 113, 134
Klepper, S., 9
Kommer, M. M., 141
Kristiansen, C. M., 86

Laurin, U., 5, 56, 68, 85
Lawler, E. E., 55
Lea, S. E. G., 15
Levin, E. J., 6
Lewis, A., 3, 13, 14, 15, 16, 17
Liebrand, W. B. G., 20, 44, 73, 103, 106
Loftus, E. F., 82
Long, S. B., 3, 9, 15, 85, 112, 113, 128, 136, 140, 141, 142, 143
Lowrey, H. M., 59, 85
Lundstedt, S. B., 56, 57

McClelland, G. M., 10, 130
McCrohan, K. F., 33
McKee, T. C., 1, 130, 136
Mackscheidt, K., 42
Maital, S., 4, 10, 11, 39, 40, 41, 42, 48, 50, 51, 57, 58
Manstead, A. S. R., 34
March, J. G., 81
Masling, J., 45
Mason, R., 8, 56, 58, 59, 68, 85
Medanik, L., 34
Messere, K. C., 24, 25
Milgram, S., 45
Milliron, V. C., 10, 12, 57, 58, 59
Montador, R. B., 7, 26
Montgomery, H., 89
Murray, M. N., 135

Nagin, D., 9
Neal, A. G., 59, 73
Nichols, D. R., 82
Norem-Heibesen, A. A., 20

Oort Commission, 135
Orleans, S., 7, 36
Orne, M. T., 45, 117
Owens, J. P., 24, 25

Perrson, A.-L., 89
Potter, J., 53
Phillips, D. L., 34
Platt, C. J., 24
Plumley, A., 83
Poole, A., 32
Prest, A. R., 6, 27

Raj, S. P., 44
Reckers, P. M., 13, 18, 19

Reiss, M., 68
Rettig, S., 59
Reynolds, K. D., 13, 18, 19
Rijsman, J. B., 55, 57, 58, 63, 70, 76
Robben, H. S. J., 5, 6, 23, 32, 34, 35, 37, 38, 79, 111, 113, 123, 138
Robins, L. N., 34
Rokeach, M., 88, 89
Rosa, P. J., 6
Rose, R., 23
Roth, A. E., 39
Royal Commission on Taxation, 2
Rundquist, E. A., 70
Rutenberg, A., 39, 40, 41, 42, 48, 50, 51, 58

Sabine, B. E. V., 1
Samuelson, S. O., 141
Sandford, C. T., 15
Sandmo, A., 8, 9, 81
Schadewald, M. S., 10, 12, 83
Schmölders, G., 23, 24, 28
Scholz, J. T., 81, 82
Schultz, J. J., 82
Schulze, W. D., 10, 44, 130
Schwartz, R. D., 7, 9, 36, 53, 113
Scott, W. J., 8, 33, 56
Sechrest, L., 53
Sharp, K., 1
Shaw, G. K., 135
Silverman, I., 40
Simon, H. A., 81
Sleeking, S, 42, 43
Slemrod, J., 15, 31, 32, 85
Sletto, R. F., 70
Slorum, N., 15
Smith, K. W., 10, 12, 13, 15, 17, 29, 47, 82, 113, 134
Smith, R., 18
Smith, S., 4, 5, 136
Smith, V. L., 39
Sobell, L. C., 33
Sparks, R., 34
Spicer, M. W., 9, 40, 50, 52, 56, 57, 62, 77, 83
Srole, L., 70, 73
Stalans, L. J., 113
Stephens, R., 34
Strøm, S., 141
Sudman, S., 34
Sullivan, D. H., 6
Swingen, J. A., 1, 3, 15, 85, 112, 113, 128, 136, 140, 141, 142, 143

Tajfel, H., 40
Tanzi, V., 4, 30
Tarpy, R. M., 15
Tedeschi, J. T., 68
Tetlock, P. E., 34
Thomas, J. E., 9, 40, 50
Toornvliet, L. G., 73
Tversky, A., 10, 11, 12, 47, 54, 79, 82, 140

Uecker, W. C., 44, 47, 102
Ulph, D. T., 6
US Bureau of the Census, 6

Van Bijsterveld, W. J., 5
Van der Pligt, J., 15, 46, 112
Van Eck, R., 4, 6, 8, 58
Van Raaij, W. F., 18
Van Veldhoven, G. M., 5, 13, 17, 58, 59, 85
Van Zon, I., 59
Verlind, W. F. M., 23
Vogel, J., 8, 17, 58, 85, 137

Waara, R., 89
Walerud, B., 5, 33, 56, 58, 62, 85, 92
Wallschutzky, I. G., 31, 36, 85
Walsh, D., 32
Wärneryd, K.-E., 5, 17, 33, 56, 58, 62, 85, 92
Watson, D., 19
Weaver, F. M., 81
Webb, E. J., 53, 131
Webley, P., 9, 15, 41, 43, 47, 50, 52, 55, 78, 111, 114, 123, 124, 126
Weck, H., 30, 31, 75
Weigel, R. H., 13, 17, 19, 21, 22, 36, 39, 54, 56, 58, 59, 60, 68, 69, 71, 73, 75, 76, 77, 79, 80, 82, 92, 109, 110, 112, 131, 137, 143
Wetherall, M., 53
Wilde, L. L., 9, 113
Willemse, H. M., 73
Witte, A. D., 9, 85, 113
Wolfe, A. C., 34
Woodbury, D. F., 9, 85, 113
Wright, J., 1

Zeller, R. A., 73
Zuckerman, M., 73

For EU product safety concerns, contact us at Calle de José Abascal, 56–1°,
28003 Madrid, Spain or eugpsr@cambridge.org.

 www.ingramcontent.com/pod-product-compliance
Ingram Content Group UK Ltd.
Pitfield, Milton Keynes, MK11 3LW, UK
UKHW010048140625
459647UK00012BB/1676